We've got a life

We've Got a Life

How people with learning difficulties have discovered who they are and claimed back their lives

Sue Deeley, Julie Smith,
Pat Black and Andy Smith

Getta Life Ltd
www.gettalifeonline.co.uk

Diversity Matters Ltd
www.diversity-matters.co.uk

We've Got a Life

Published by Getta Life Ltd
www.gettalifeonline.co.uk

Copyright © 2016 Getta Life and Diversity Matters

British Library Cataloguing in Publication Data
A record is available from the British Library

First published 2016

All UK rights reserved. No part of this publication may be reproduced, stored in a retrieval system, or transmitted, in any form or by any means, electronic, mechanical, photocopying, recording or otherwise, except as expressly permitted by law, without the prior, written permission of the publisher.

For further information and enquiries:

    Getta Life Ltd
    E-mail: gettalifeadmin@btconnect.com
    Website: www. gettalifeonline.co.uk

    Diversity Matters
    E-mail: diverad@diversity-matters.co.uk
    Website: www.diversity-matters.co.uk

Book and cover design by Sarah McCall

Edited by Jack Richardson of True 2 Self and
Dea Parkin of Fiction Feedback

Line drawings by Kate Westhead

ISBN: 978-0-9935088-0-6

The most precious gift we can
offer anyone is our attention.
When mindfulness embraces those
we love, they will bloom like flowers.

Thich Nhat Hanh

This copy of
We've Got a Life
is presented to:

....

Contents

Chapter 1	It's About Everyone	3
Chapter 2	Relationships	15
Chapter 3	From There to Here – Real Lives	41
Chapter 4	How Circles and Teams Reflect the Person	57
Chapter 5	Discovery	77
Chapter 6	Purpose and Intent	99
Chapter 7	Community	121
Chapter 8	Safety, Security and Healing	139
Chapter 9	Celebration and Belonging	165
Chapter 10	Are Getta Life Doing What They Say?	181

Acknowledgements

A book about Hope, Love, Moving forward, Growth and Healing. It demonstrates a style of support that enables people to be truly themselves. We want to acknowledge and appreciate the work done by John O'Brien, Connie Lyle O'Brien, Beth Mount, Michael Smull, Dave Hingsburger and David Pitonyak who have greatly influenced our practice and taught us how to be person-centred.

Chapter 1

It's About Everyone

Written by Pat Black of Diversity Matters

I am writing this chapter immediately after the Getta Life Oscars Night celebration. The event was about everyone, it was a fantastic fun party; moving, celebratory and very well organised. It symbolises the Getta Life quality, the heart of the organisation that is hard to put into words but might be something like 'Everybody matters'; everyone is an exceptional human being and everyone is different. It's the job of Getta Life to support each unique individual to emerge and become more themselves. This is not rhetoric, nor is it only in relation to the people supported. On Oscars night each and every one of the people working in or supported by the organisation was awarded a Getta Life Oscar.

Sue and Julie read out and presented an award to each of the people they support. These weren't the only rewards; the team managers also presented an award to each staff member.

Each award was a thank you to people for being who they are and a recognition of what they've achieved. The entire evening was incredible; people who have never or very rarely had the opportunity to dress up shopped for new clothes, had their hair done and wore make-up. Men who have only worn casual clothes for years turned up looking incredibly smart and proud of their appearance. People who struggle to be in large groups stayed for hours, receiving their awards with looks of pride and happiness. It was clear that people knew this was all about them.

The culture of the organisation showed in the whole evening – the attention to detail meant that everyone was included because everyone matters. There were proud families present, some who said they would never have imagined that their son or daughter would be taking part in this sort of event and receiving an award. More mundanely but at least as important in the sense of attention to detail was the meal planning. Dinner was provided and the choice was meat or vegetable lasagne with salad and potato wedges. That might seem insignificant but it was a very, very important detail. It meant that everyone had the same food to eat, and as it was soft it was easy to cut up and everyone could eat it regardless of whether they had teeth or not. It was also very well prepared and followed by an individual strawberry cheesecake – again an easy-to-eat choice.

This is what this chapter is about – Sue and Julie believe that everyone is important and have created an organisational culture where almost everyone knows that they are valued and important. Those who don't know they're important will gradually find out that they are and that they matter to Getta Life. Not only the people supported, not only the staff or the families: everyone is important and everyone matters. It seems to us that this is a crucial element in making this organisation so successful. It's not easy to do and needs constant vigilance, but it is the only way to ensure truly person-centred support provision. No organisation should expect staff to treat the people they support well if it doesn't treat the staff in the same way.

So what follows are a number of stories that speak for themselves. The main points are summarised at the end.

Staff stories

Becky

Becky joined Getta Life as a relief worker – a role which she enjoyed, but she came to a point where she asked Julie for a place to belong. Julie listened and Becky was offered a permanent job. She started work in the team supporting Angela and quickly realised that it wasn't the same as relief work at all; there was a difference between working with 'a client' and a person you support: *'When you work for a client you do a shift and go home, but when you support someone you make a relationship and bind yourself to them.'* So when she moved to work permanently with Angela and her partner Daniel, Becky says her whole life changed. As Becky became involved with them she also became part of their person-centred plan, and seeing how positive their future could be, she started to become positive about her own life too.

She saw that Daniel and Angela had something special; they were in love and cared deeply for one another and that showed Becky how this was missing in her own life. She felt inspired and opened up to the possibility of change; she says this helped her to meet her new husband. Becky describes Getta Life as helping her to work differently; to respect the people she supports, to become part of their lives and form relationships that make everyone happy. She missed them when she wasn't at work.

This may seem straightforward but it reveals a different way of thinking about people who use support. The second part of the story shows how the organisation really has to be about everyone and that includes the staff. Often organisations encourage staff to be present for people and to feel that their work with people is more than a job, but then they don't extend that care in turn to the staff. The next part of Becky's story demonstrates this care.

Becky also talks about a very difficult period of her life when she was detained because of her immigration status. She heard a statement from her employers, Getta Life, read out in court saying that she did her job very well; this had a profound effect and sustained Becky through her detention. After she was released she sorted out her status but didn't think she would be allowed to come back to Getta Life; she felt she had betrayed their trust. A friend passed on how Becky felt and Sue texted Becky and invited her back. Becky couldn't believe it and returned to work at Getta Life. She explains that she entered the job with all of her heart, eventually returning to Angela and Daniel's team as a manager. Since moving on to another team where she also very much enjoys the work she is able to say:

> 'Daniel and Angela have made me the person I am today and I am proud to be their friend. Sue and Julie planted a seed in me and I have grown to be a different person. This job has improved me and now I am a better person; the work comes from deep, deep down inside me and I am thankful for the trust Sue and Julie have shown in me. They have supported my training in counselling and that's also improved my management skills. I keep growing and changing and I'm going to teach listening skills to support workers in the company. I feel appreciated by Sue and Julie, and so when they ask me to do something I am happy to do it.'

Gari

Gari joined Getta Life in 2003 having been introduced to Getta Life by a friend; he was so nervous that he arrived for his interview an hour and a half early. After the interview he walked all the way home thinking he'd made a blunder. He couldn't believe it when he was offered the job and told he did a fantastic interview. This was Gari's first job in support work; he was shy, quiet and not very confident. He found it very hard to write in English as this isn't his first language.

He started learning about the people he supported – Sandra, Philip and Sarah – and a whole different scenario opened up to him. Sally, the team manager, helped Gari get to know Sandra, and Philip and Sarah worked with him to help him learn. Gari talks about this process in a very matter-of-fact way and what he says is very powerful.

> *'Philip doesn't communicate with sounds but he is a man like me and must have similar things to say, so I had to figure out how to understand. It took me a couple of years to get to know him and then I couldn't wait to get to work. Philip taught me a lot of things I needed to learn and helped me develop how I worked with people. I was comfortable with my life and had no thought of developing myself, but I saw Philip developing his life and said to myself, why am I not developing too? I could see a big difference in Philip and how he was and I knew that I could do more too.'*

Gari went on to explain that Sue and Julie always say, *'You can't say you can't do something unless you try it.'* He has seen that they never give up on anyone and are not judgmental.

When Gari joined Getta Life he explained that he left school when he was very young to look after his family and so never thought he would be able to achieve much, but he took those messages from Sue and Julie to heart and tried to live his life like that too. When he explained that he was not good at writing, a part of him expected to be told that he would have to leave, but instead Getta Life offered him the opportunity to go to college. When he left the meeting, he cried. Then he went to college and pushed himself.

A little later the Getta Life men's group needed a leader and Gari thought maybe he should do it, but he was nervous – so nervous that when Sue was coming round to the house he would get Philip ready and they'd go out so she couldn't ask him to lead it. Then he remembered how they'd supported him and he got his courage together and said, *'OK, I'll do it, I* will *lead the men's group.'* Gari continued, *'They said that I needed to put my ideas together and make a presentation to them. I did that and they were impressed and said I could try it. I decided I would really make it work and I have. I'm proud of what I did.'*

When the opportunity arose to become a manager, Sue encouraged Gari to apply. He says he was very nervous because he really wanted the job and was delighted when successful. He says,

> 'It's amazing to do this job and I'm still learning and growing. I realised I didn't know myself as well as I thought when I went on the bereavement training. I thought I was tough but through the training I've learnt to deal with it properly. The listening-skills training has helped me to be a better manager. Sue and Julie let you be yourself, and that really helps – if I have a problem I don't hide it. Working here, the sky's the limit. Getta Life is for everyone, not only the service users. They help everyone's dreams come true. I never imagined I would have a job at this level. Sue and Julie embrace everyone, they appreciate us all and say "thank you for your work", and they're able to see the exceptional in everyone. They just don't know how good they are.'

Gari has proved himself to be one of Getta Life's best and most loyal members of staff.

Catherine
Catherine, like Becky, started work with Getta Life as a relief worker and says the difference between Getta Life and other organisations is that Getta Life is a place where the more you give the more you get. She eventually joined Jonathan and Zara's team as a permanent worker and felt like she was at home. She has seen huge changes in what Zara is able to do for herself and in her improving health. Catherine is a very new team manager and says that she feels supported by the confidence Julie has in her. She is learning lots of new skills and feels supported; she has attended training on how to be a manager and feels she's constantly learning and growing. She says she's learning to present issues in ways that are positive, and that has changed her. She's beginning to get faster at noticing things and dealing with them. The whole experience has been a challenge that has meant she's had to grow up, take bumps, and get up again and face things head on. Catherine says she knows she can sit down

with Julie or Sue and discuss difficulties without feeling she has failed; they help her to handle things but don't take over. Her peers are very supportive too. She has realised that she and the team possess a lot of knowledge and information about Jonathan and Zara and that they have a responsibility to share it with professionals and to stay in charge.

Agnes

Agnes tells her own story:

> 'What makes Getta Life different is that Sue and Julie are always telling us to reflect, look back and try to improve. We see the way they work, we see the way we work, and that is the Getta Life way. Now that I'm working with a new team I'm teaching them the Getta Life way. People need to learn that the person we support is an individual and we talk about them in positive ways. We are walking on a journey together. We're listening to them and trying to understand them better. I love explaining things to new people. I wasn't a confident person when I started but I have grown. Sue and Julie have shown confidence in me and have taught me to do what's right all the time. Neither of them shies away from telling the truth, even when it's difficult; they don't sugar-coat it, nor do they turn a blind eye.
>
> They would never cover anything up or say it's OK if it isn't; that's important because they have a vision and they stick to it completely. They know no one is perfect and that people are all different and they accept these differences.
>
> No company offers more training. I've done a degree in Social Care at the Open University – they just said, "You enjoy your job so why not do a course?". I'm going on to do a Masters at Warwick University.
>
> Sue and Julie have taught me to be hopeful. I didn't believe people could change but I have seen people change simply because they have been treated positively. I have changed myself and I've learnt that support work is not only giving, it's taking too. Each person gives you a lot back.'

Irene

Irene worked very well and positively with Jonathan and Zara for many years and helped instigate some very positive changes for them. Recently, Julie could see by her appraisal and through supervision that Irene needed and wanted a new challenge. Particularly she wanted to learn about setting up a support service, and so Getta Life decided she could take on setting up a new service for Sally. Irene welcomed this opportunity with enthusiasm, but when it was discussed in the team meeting Jonathan made an upset noise, a kind of moan, and everyone realised that he didn't want Irene to leave. The team were supportive of Jonathan, helping him to understand why Irene needed to do this and helping him to know the new team manager as well as working with Irene to stay in touch.

This is important because the way with which this was dealt shows that everyone matters; in this situation both Jonathan and Irene matter. Jonathan is part of the discussion, his reactions are heard and noticed and he is supported with the change. Irene is also important and a new challenge is right for her, so Jonathan had to be supported to express his feelings and helped to let Irene go as a staff member and re-negotiate his continuing relationswhip with her.

Getta Life also acknowledges that not everyone needs or wants to move on to different levels or to grow more. If people are at a level that is good enough for them and the job they're doing then they don't need to be pushed, but equally organisations need to notice when someone wants to develop, and to encourage them.

Staff training

The stories above all illustrate this point. People are undertaking many different kinds of training but each course suits the needs of the person, both in terms of their personal growth and in supporting their role within the organisation. Through reflective supervision meetings, people are encouraged to pay attention to how their learning impacts on their work. It's easy to see if the training or course is the right one for the person – if it is, then they're excited and talk about it at work.

Offering training that meets an individual's needs and will enhance their work

---

Walking the talk

Many people have talked about the difference they see and how Getta Life's work is truly person-centred. Family, friends, staff and fellow professionals are clear that in Getta Life 'everyone matters' means exactly that. There is not much comparison between Getta Life and other providers. Stories so far are about individuals. People see that it's different right away, that words translate into actions and that the people who are supported and the staff alike are truly all seen as important.

A staff member's insight

Staff member Daud commented how he felt that in Getta Life the walk matches the talk. Now a team manager, he sees how the training is put together and understands why so much emphasis is put on it. Daud is now studying, and as he learns, the more he understands why we do things the way we do.

> *'Getta Life is not like other places. If you don't know something you can ask for help, it's lovely.*
>
> *As a manager I've sometimes used the wrong platform and said, "Sue said this needs to happen", but now I realise this is my responsibility. So now I say, "This is wrong, let's talk about it," or "If you were getting this support how would you want it to happen?"*
>
> *And I learnt this from Sue: don't put difficult things off but do them right away.'*

CHAPTER 1
It's About Everyone

KEY MESSAGES

- ☑ Values apply to everyone.
- ☑ Recognise that everyone is an exceptional human being and everyone is different.
- ☑ Offer practical procedures that everyone can learn.
- ☑ Grow a culture of not blaming, but of reflection and learning when things go wrong.
- ☑ Be the change you want to see, and then model the required behaviour throughout the whole organisation and walk the talk.
- ☑ Support the staff to grow and learn.
- ☑ Ensure all staff are clear about what the job is and what needs to be done.
- ☑ Invest in people.
- ☑ Honesty should be truly valued, and in the present.

Chapter 2

Relationships

Written by Sue Deeley of Getta Life

Relationships are what matter in life; when they're right everything else is more likely to be right

Any new relationship starts with hope, excitement, maybe some trepidation, and generally two people who have chosen to be there. This is very different for the people we support. They are expected to have relationships with people who very often they've not chosen; they have a lot of experience of poor, transient relationships, poor support experiences, maybe abusive relationships and certainly relationships where there is inequality in power. Some of the messages that they've learnt about relationships might be that it's OK for people to hurt you; that people come and go; and that it's not worth getting close to someone as you may get hurt. As a support worker you need to understand what has gone before in the person's life so that you can work on developing a relationship together in a sensitive way that helps the person learn a new script.

As the support worker, you may need to learn a new script too. If you come to work believing it's wrong to be in a personal relationship with the person you support or that people with learning difficulties don't understand or can't be in relationships, then it won't be possible to be in the right relationship with the person you support. Not sure this is true? Read on.

All of us have a universal need to be loved and liked. You can't be loved or liked unless you're in a relationship with people. People can cope with most things in life if they have someone alongside in the right relationship with them. Some of the people we support were very lonely and isolated when we first met them; some appeared not to be in a relationship with anyone.

Three examples of relationship building

Here are three examples. Matthew, who was especially isolated, was formerly seen as a problem and had a huge reputation for being difficult to support. He was frightened of people and spent as much time as possible trying to be invisible. He was seen as almost not human. Once he was supported by Getta Life, he often refused to get dressed and hurt himself to a point that was very distressing, pulling his ears until they bled and not letting us touch them to clean them. His ears became infected and hurt him as a result, leading to more self-harming, and so the cycle continued. It is difficult to write more of his story as it's too painful and sad to put down on paper. It's made me very careful in my work with Matthew and I work extremely hard not to repeat any of the past. We make sure any new members of his team know and understand his story so they can appreciate the responsibility they have to get it right with him, and to work hard at developing a kind, respectful, nurturing relationship to support his healing.

Patrick was very uncomfortable around people and simply treated us like objects that he moved around. When he got stressed he would make us leave his home and wait outside on the doorstep until he wanted to let us in again.

Sarah was invisible in the place she lived before she moved into her own home. She was often put to sit in a chair in a second lounge far away from the other people she lived with because sometimes she would shout. When we first met Sarah she sat with her head down, often alone for hours at a time, unable to move because she uses a wheelchair and needs support to do so. Sarah frequently cried and very seldom looked at people.

Most of the hurt, distress and damage that people like Matthew, Patrick and Sarah have suffered is because they haven't been in good relationships with the people around them. Those people supporting them either didn't bother to get to know them or saw them as less than human, so didn't see the need to be in a relationship. If the person was perceived as less than human, it became easy to abuse and hurt them. It has been a massive leap of faith for the people we support to take the risk and get into a relationship with the person supporting them and let other people be close to them again. Yet if people don't do this they are unable to grow and will stay empty, hurt, distressed and angry. Most people take time to trust people and to know someone; if you've been abused or hurt it takes even longer; if you also have a learning difficulty it may take even longer.

It took three and a half years of careful one-to-one relationship-building to get Matthew off his sofa and taking tentative steps back into the real world. The work to support Matthew over this period involved a lot of considered, gentle persuasion and encouragement. We started by making sure all the team understood the importance of Matthew being in control, of not forcing him to do anything and of waiting until he was ready to rejoin the world. We thought of ways to help him to feel included and curious about what went on outside his home so he might be tempted on a good day to go out and see what was happening. Initially it might take all day to persuade him to get dressed and go to his car, then he would refuse to go any further; gradually over time he has got braver. The important thing was to go at Matthew's pace and enable him to decide how much he could manage and when he could participate in things. Matthew needed to know it was worth the effort, so the team talked to him frequently about what was going on in the world and suggested things he might like to try. The team always gave him lots of appreciation and encouragement whenever he tried to explore a little beyond his home. Importantly, they told him lots of what they liked about him and what they got from spending time with him. The combination of all these strands gave him a strong message that we believed in both him and his capacity to heal and recover.

Trust – the foundation of relationships

Sally is another person Getta Life cares for. During the time we were getting to know Sally and her family it was important to rebuild her family's trust in services. For Sally's birthday we had a bouncy castle and barbecue; it was fantastic fun and a pleasure to see her relaxed and enjoying herself with her family, friends and staff. Everyone had a go and Sally enjoyed watching others as well as taking part. This was a special thing for us as it was about the relationships that Getta Life staff have not only with Sally but also with her family for whom services in the past had been unacceptable and a source of anxiety and conflict.

At Getta Life, we start from the position that we trust people unless there is a reason not to. This is sometimes met with cynicism by new staff if they've worked in other organisations where trust is only in place until something goes wrong, and then it shifts to blame. We trust the people we support to be able to grow and show us how they want to lead their lives; we trust in them and so follow their lead.

Patrick knows what is right for him and we have learnt to trust his judgement even if we feel he isn't growing much. Patrick is now in his seventies and the oldest person we support; he spent many years living in an institution. He is, not surprisingly, a very anxious person who finds people difficult to be around and is very particular about how things need to be done. Patrick had little experience of everyday life when we first met him. Shopping was a challenging experience as he thought he should eat the food on the way round the supermarket. He likes to sleep with his shoes on, and to have his front door open all the time. We trusted him and supported him in all of these preferences.

Movement is how Patrick soothes himself; feeling free and able to move whenever he needs to is the most important aid to him feeling OK and enjoying life. Patrick has taught us the importance of the simple things in life: lots of long walks, long drives, good food, the local pub. We are now very excited because he has started to be in a relationship with us instead of seeing us as objects that he moved around in his home. Patrick no longer pushes us out of his house and makes us wait on the doorstep until he lets us in again. Now he looks at us, makes eye contact and sometimes makes a happy chuckling noise when he is pleased to see us. These are all little gifts and mean so much from him. We're receiving them more often as he starts to trust us more.

Gari did a magnificent job supporting Philip when he had an accident and was burnt in the bath. Philip spent a long time in the burns unit in a local hospital and Gari was a very important part of his recovery. This experience helped Philip to trust his support team more as he had to endure a lot of frightening experiences and the team were by his side all of the time.

Gari also took over running and organising the men's group and did a great job. Gari grew into a confident, charismatic, well-respected support worker who is now a team manager in Justin's team. Justin and his family trust Gari and feel safe with him. We trust Justin's family to help us get it right for Justin, and as a result that's what happens. Trust is a fundamental part of good relationships; relationships break down if trust isn't present.

Recognising that people with learning difficulties have meaningful relationships and friendships with each other, their families and their support staff
---

Daniel and Angela – building a relationship

Daniel and Angela met at a Coventry nursing home for people with learning difficulties after returning to the city from separate long-stay institutions. (For more detail, see *Chapter 3: From There to Here – Real Lives*.) A community nurse who worked with them both believed they had a special connection and should live together when the nursing home closed. We met Daniel and Angela in 2002. It was clear that they did indeed have some form of special connection but none of us understood how special it was at the time. Daniel and Angela often sat together in the same chair in the nursing home and watched what was happening from there. It was as though they provided each other with security and comfort. It was sometimes noisy, chaotic and a little scary in their nursing home so they obviously helped each other to feel safer.

Daniel and Angela moved into their own home in September 2003. It quickly became apparent that they did have a unique connection and the better we got to know them the more obvious it became that they were in love. Their level of commitment to each other was inspiring and made us realise what a lot they had to teach us about relationships, closeness and intimacy.

We began to talk at their person-centred planning days about their relationship, how it worked and how much they meant to each other. Getta Life plans contain a section where we encourage dreams for the future, and thought is given to what life choices people may have made if they didn't have a disability. When we reached this part of the plan for Daniel and Angela we talked about how proud they were about their relationship and how they may have married. We talked about how they may like to have this celebrated and their relationship recognised. We felt that they would like to do this as they are very open and proud people. Daniel's mum wasn't so sure; she felt we didn't know for certain that this is what they'd like and really it was our dream, not theirs. For several years this was a topic that we talked about at every planning day but it didn't move forward. Slowly as we learnt about the levels of intimacy between the two we had more evidence to talk about the depth of their relationship and commitment.

The other thing that changed was our eyes and how we viewed the pair. Once we were open to believing that Daniel and Angela's relationship was as real as anyone else's we began to see even more evidence to support this; our own prejudices had stopped us seeing what had always been there. We all had lots of fears about privacy, intimacy, sexuality and how the two of them understood these things. What I have learnt is that we were blind to what was right in front of us when we evaluated it in the same way that people who use words relate to each other. Daniel and Angela regularly show each other how delighted they are to see each other. If Daniel has been out without Angela she watches the window for his return and once he appears she cheers, claps, rocks backwards and forwards, smiles and laughs. This happens not only every time Daniel returns home, but also when Daniel gets up from bed each morning and any time she hasn't seen him for a while. Daniel always waits for Angela to get up before he has breakfast; he always walks just behind her wheelchair when they go out together; he cuddles her lots, they play with paper together and they tell us when they want some privacy. Again it took us some time to recognise this as we were looking with our unseeing eyes. Often Daniel will sit on the floor in front of Angela and put his head in her lap, Angela strokes his hair and sometimes they can get quite rough with each other. We used to try and stop this as we felt Angela wasn't comfortable with what was happening. However, she'd get annoyed with us when we tried to intervene and tell us off with a noise she makes when she is cross. What we tried to do then was take ourselves out of the room and give them some privacy, as when they were being intimate that was very clearly what they wanted us to do. *They* are entirely happy with how they touch each other; we had judged it and misunderstood it. We thought that they didn't understand intimacy; actually they understand completely.

Privacy is very difficult to achieve when you have twenty-four hour support. We need to think about this more, especially when people are in intimate relationships. We also realised that it was hard for Daniel's mum to understand the level of their relationship as she didn't see those intimate times and we only saw them because of the couple's support needs. Most mothers don't know the details of their sons' relationships but when you communicate using words, mums can check if their son is happy and OK. Daniel's mum didn't have that way of checking. It was a big leap of faith for her to believe us and begin to comprehend it. This is more than understandable given that intimacy between two people with severe learning difficulties remains one of the biggest taboos in our society.

Daniel and Angela celebrated their relationship with a ceremony at their local church; they have been part of the church community since they moved into their own home. The vicar knew them well and had developed a good understanding of them and their support team. Daniel's mum was clear about how she wanted the day to go and we knew she didn't want it to be a big formal occasion. Angela's sister was comfortable to go along with whatever arrangements were made as long as they were right for Angela and Daniel.

The day arrived, 6 October 2008. It was as you would expect: lots of nerves and lots of excitement. I was having my usual last-minute panic about what if we'd got it all wrong and what if it didn't make sense to Daniel and Angela. Looking back I had misjudged them again as they didn't put a foot wrong all day. There could be no doubt for anyone present that both Daniel and Angela understood what was happening, were proud of the day and participated in beautiful style. Highlights of the day were:

- Angela walking downstairs in her dress like a princess, never stepping on the hem and standing regally, wearing make-up and not rubbing it off and leaving the sparkly beads and gems in her hair. She looked stunning all day and clearly loved being the centre of attention.
- Daniel smiling and waiting patiently in his suit while Angela was getting dressed.
- Daniel and Angela's attentiveness when the vicar blessed their relationship and talked about what he knew of them.
- Daniel moving between his mum and Angela throughout the ceremony, quietly taking care of the two most important women in his life.
- Angela's excitement as they exchanged gifts.
- Holding huge bunches of balloons outside the church while the photos were taken.
- Daniel sitting between his mum and Angela at the meal afterwards, leaning back in his chair, chest pushed out and beaming his smile; he was so very proud.

The following weekend we had a great big party for everyone to come together with Daniel and Angela to celebrate their relationship. A lot of thought was put into this evening and everyone in Getta Life got very excited about it. The impact it has had on the whole of the organisation has been immense. Some of our best staff didn't believe it was possible when we talked about helping Daniel and Angela to have their relationship blessed at their church and this made us think that maybe we needed some training regarding relationships. We needed to make sure we weren't missing other important connections, relationships and friendships.

Some highlights of the party night were:

- Everyone arriving before Daniel and Angela at the venue and waiting patiently for them to arrive. A feat in itself for people who for very good reasons struggle to wait.
- Everyone bringing Daniel and Angela wedding presents.
- Everyone including support staff dressed for a wedding.
- The spontaneous applause from everyone when Matthew arrived and managed to be part of his friend's special evening.
- The celebration cake that we had helped Matthew make for Daniel and Angela set on three tiers and looking very professional.
- The sense of joy from everyone all evening.
- Daniel and Angela's immense pride and happiness.
- What great fun the whole evening was, how proud I was to work for Getta Life and how proud I felt of everyone we support and all of our staff.

Staff training on building relationships

There is a lot of emphasis on training in Getta Life. It is not acceptable for staff to miss training and Julie, my fellow director, and I attend all training and deliver a lot of it. This means staff are very clear about their roles and what is expected of them. Right from induction training, support staff are told that they're expected to be in a relationship with the person they support and that they have to work at that level all the time. It's not enough to give good support but no heart. A lot of Getta Life staff are from Africa. They often talk about doing things from their hearts. At first I found this a bit too gushy and felt uncomfortable with the phrase. Now I know that to support people from my heart is absolutely the right thing to do. Often new staff who have worked in other support organisations struggle with this concept as they've been told it's unprofessional. Our view is that it is potentially hurtful and unprofessional *not* to be in a good relationship with the person you support. Our role is to ensure those relationships stay positive and safe. The people we support have lived with many labels and many experiences of being treated as inhuman; to be in a relationship makes you human. It is much more difficult to hurt someone you know and are in a relationship with. We would argue that good, close relationships with the person you support protect the person as well as making the role of support worker much more enjoyable.

Effective training is crucial to give support staff the chance to work out the ingredients of a good relationship, in relation to the person they support, their families, their friends and their teams. We provide specific training about the right relationship, emotional literacy, loving relationships and friendships. We talk about relationships in team meetings and observe relationships developing and changing.

> **We all need to learn about relationships and think about them. Good training about relationships is crucial**

Karl used to be very anxious, loud, and slept very little. He was quite hard to be with when we started to support him. He was so worried that he rarely enjoyed the moment unless it involved loud music. Now I watch Karl in his team meeting showing his support staff what he wants. I hear touching stories about him waiting patiently in the bank, waiting for his prescription in the chemist's and waiting for the right bus. At first Karl wouldn't wait in the bank if it was busy and there was a queue. If the staff wouldn't serve him first he sat on the floor and screamed loudly, or left just as he got to the front of the queue. The staff in the bank and the chemist's have all commented on how much Karl has changed. His family is very impressed by his developing patience. I am sure that this has all come about because Karl really likes the three people who currently support him. I know they really like him; they get excited about his progress and see infinite possibilities for him.

Daniel and Angela have also helped support staff to learn about the importance of relationships. They have been co-trainers on the training about close, loving relationships and friendships. Their team has helped them to tell their story using photos, and the team themselves have shared their experiences of learning from Daniel and Angela. Robert, who supports Daniel, says his relationship with his own partner has improved immensely since he started to support Daniel. Daniel has shown him how to be particularly sensitive towards a woman, how to be patient, kind and generally more considerate. Staff in other teams get very excited on the training because they begin to see that the person they support might one day find romance or develop more intimate friendships.

Daniel has been helped to tell the story of how his friendship has helped Matthew to get braver and rejoin the world. Since this training, Alice and Matthew have developed a close friendship and spend time together each week. This came about through support staff noticing that Matthew seemed to feel safe around Alice and the two liked similar things. Both teams thought it was worth helping Alice and Matthew to spend time together to see if they enjoyed each other's company. Matthew's team describe his excitement when he is going to see her; he smiles as he is getting ready to go to her house and his tummy-rubbing and smiling show his clear enjoyment when they are together.

Zara and Karl have developed a close relationship too. Karl gets quite shy and bashful when we talk about his relationship with Zara and goes very quiet. When he visits Zara he always has to stay for a cup of tea and he looks at her very closely. Zara has developed a bit of a strut and obviously feels beautiful. For Karl and Zara this is a lovely new experience and even if the relationship doesn't work for ever they have both tasted something very different to the relationships they've had so far in their lives.

These relationships wouldn't have developed if support staff hadn't noticed when people seemed interested in each other. When people don't have words to communicate it's important to follow the clues, try things and note the person's response. If it works, do it again; if it doesn't, try a few more times with different approaches and perhaps better support. If it isn't working after this then it's probably not the right thing.

> **Everyone in the organisation, the families and friends of the people we support need to be in a good relationship to make it work**

The following stories all illustrate this point in their diverse ways.

Justin

When we started to support Justin it was quite difficult to find the right approach; Justin was highly anxious and his family were feeling distrustful and let down by support agencies. We were determined to get it right as we knew it had already gone wrong for him several times. Two support services had given notice and we didn't want to cause Justin or his family any more harm or distress. When I first met Justin's dad to talk about how we could support Justin, he listened politely and quietly. When I'd finished telling him about Getta Life he said, 'Well, that all sounds great, but with respect you are the third person from an organisation like yours saying the same things. So far we've been let down. You seem a nice person but we'll see what happens.'

Justin's dad invited me to follow him and Justin one day when they went out to town together so that I could see how he supports him. The idea was that I should 'accidentally' meet up with them in a café in town for a cup of tea. This seemed like a strange thing to do but it felt as though Justin's dad wanted to show me how to support Justin, and as he felt he had not been heard in the past I thought it was a good idea to go. It was a very odd experience following Justin and his dad into town as they popped in and out of shops and then acting surprised when we met in the café and joining them for a cup of tea. However, I learnt loads. Crucially, I saw that Justin's dad had absolute faith in Justin and Justin trusted his dad implicitly. I began to get some idea of Justin's level of anxiety as I could hear his dad giving him a constant running commentary and providing reassurance even during their short trip to town. Now I know Justin well, it's clear to us that his dad and mum are the Justin experts. They can always help us, guide us and offer both us and Justin support if we're struggling to get it right. Justin is very quick to pick up on any tension or conflict so it's a crucial part of his support to get on well with his mum and dad. They had a reputation in the same way that Justin did; both reputations were undeserved and say far more about poor support than about Justin and his family.

Beware of reputations because frequently that's all they are; they're often far from the reality. We have worked carefully to develop good relationships between everyone in Justin's life. Part of this consisted in recruiting and keeping a stable staff group around him to enable natural relationships to develop. We also made sure that we kept Justin's mum and dad informed about everything when we started to support him, even when it was bad news. We had an incident where a staff member got quite seriously hurt; it was important that they knew about this but also that they and Justin weren't made to feel as though they were to blame. In fact our learning from that incident was that there was too much shared anxiety between the staff and Justin, leading to him feeling unsafe and then acting in a way that was unsafe. We now know that all staff, at all times must be calm, strong and confident in themselves and in Justin for it to work. We ensure that we make time to talk to Justin's mum and dad when there is good news as well as difficulties. We now have a relationship that is based on trust and mutual respect and this makes it easier to support Justin and to ensure that we're getting it right for him.

We have however experienced a time when things went wrong. There was a serious incident when Justin was hurt by a member of his team when they were supporting him. This was hard because it was damaging to trust and everyone was feeling sad and let down. We trust our colleagues to work well and from the heart, and largely this is what people do, but sometimes they don't and this is when it can become unsafe. It was hard for Justin's mum and dad to feel OK about letting Justin return to our support and it was a big leap of faith for everyone to heal and to get back to being in a good relationship again. I reflected that where it's a real relationship when things are going well it's deeply joyful and feels good, but it's equally painful and hard when we're trying to put things right after they've gone wrong. Trust takes a long time to build and can be very quickly damaged; you have to hope that the foundations of trust are strong enough and solid enough to be able to rebuild and hopefully get strong again. Justin's mum said this is the thing that all parents are scared of when they let their vulnerable child leave home and be cared for by someone else. We felt and feel terrible that on this occasion we let them down. It made us take a hard look at our checks and controls and change an already rigorous assessment process to do everything possible to prevent it happening again.

Catherine
Sadly a member of staff, Gladys, died from cancer. Gladys had been supporting Catherine for a long time and it was a very sad time for her. While Gladys was ill we took Catherine to visit her – this was a big thing for Catherine as she's very uncomfortable in hospitals and we knew it took courage for her to do this.

When Gladys died, Catherine went to see her family to express her sympathy and she also went to Gladys's memorial service. It was clear to see the impact that Gladys had had in Catherine's life and the affection that Catherine held for her.

Neil
Some time ago Neil's grandparents began to find it too hard for him to visit them at their home due to the size of his new wheelchair and his reducing mobility. It was important to everyone that Neil and his grandparents continued to have time together and so Neil's team supported him in picking up his grandparents every Friday and taking them out. The team spent more and more time with Neil and his grandparents and the trust and friendship that developed has been rewarding for all involved. They've been to many new places, like garden centres and pubs and on country walks and even to wheelchair basketball. They've learnt about each other's life stories and taught each other things along the way. Most importantly, the team have had an amazing insight into Neil's story.

> **The relationship between the person being supported and the support worker must be the right relationship. Support workers must like the person they are supporting**

Neil began to invite his grandma to theatre evenings with him and has also taken out his grandad and his cousin Alex. Recently they went to a barbeque at Neil's church and were excited to see how well known and liked he is there. All of these events help us to know that we're getting the support right for Neil; they ensure Neil has a full family life and knows how much he is loved. It also gives confidence to his grandparents that the team who support him are committed to him and understand him well. It's all about trust.

Sarah

Sarah and Promila, her support worker, have a beautiful relationship based on mutual respect, trust and a tangible love for each other. They enjoy spending time together and have a unique bond that the rest of Sarah's team admire and envy. Sarah makes a special sound when she sees Promila, leans in close to her and is clearly very happy whenever they're together. Promila talks about Sarah being part of her family and says as long as she can support her to be happy, she is happy. Promila understands that helping Sarah to be happy is her role in life and takes great pride and satisfaction from achieving this; she says it doesn't feel like work and she can't imagine doing anything else.

Karl

'Reflective exercises' are essential items at Karl's team meetings. Peter, who supports Karl, talked recently in a reflective exercise about how easy his work is now because he knows Karl, likes him and enjoys spending time with him. It's obvious that they like each other and that they have lots of fun together. Peter talked about how it was hard at first as he didn't understand Karl and Karl didn't know or trust Peter. Doing things together was difficult as Karl would be too anxious to stay still long enough to experience whatever they were doing together. Peter said that what helped him was the rest of the team telling him about Karl and helping him to understand him. You have to like someone if you're going to spend thirty-five hours per week exclusively with that one person. Karl had experience of a support worker who didn't like him or enjoy spending time with him; she said she did but her behaviour suggested otherwise. As a result Karl was always anxious, loud, and hard to support when she was with him. It was a challenge to get her to see that it was as much about her as about Karl. Her view was that Karl needed to learn to be different; our view is that Karl is just fine as he is, and we like him and enjoy spending time with him as he is. Fairly quickly this support worker realised that working with one person was not her thing and moved back into a more traditional care setting where there is less intimacy.

Mark

Mark is quite new to Getta Life; he moved into his new home in July last year. At first he was very anxious and tested the staff's resolve, needing lots of reassurance that they were really listening to him and were there for him in a way that made him feel liked and secure. At first I struggled to find the right relationship with Mark as I found it hard to be natural with him, and because of my struggle I thought the team might be finding it tricky too; indeed at first we all were. This was because Mark felt the need to pretend to be someone other than himself. In the past he'd been made to feel invisible and unimportant so now he had a deep need to be important and listened to; this meant he was often very formal and stilted. However, we're all now in the right relationship with Mark: all different relationships but all good. Mark sees his team as his friends, and me as 'Getta Life who works in the office'! Mark often talks about having his own team of support workers or 'my key workers' and about the pleasure of having his own home and not needing to move again. Mark loves the status and importance he gains from having both his own home and a much more personalised style of support. In a recent team meeting we conducted an exercise to discover what we appreciated about working with him. I was moved by everyone's response. Daud took Mark's hand and looked into his eyes and spoke for five minutes about all the things he enjoyed about being with him; how welcoming and appreciative he is. Edgar talked about Mark's great sense of humour, his jokes and how much fun they have together, and also about how adventurous he is. Luxson talked about how much he was enjoying being a support worker and how he looked forward to coming to work; he particularly enjoys learning to cook with Mark. I love knowing Mark because he's funny, great fun to be with, always looking to try new things and wants to live life to the full. Once I understood Mark more and knew him better I discovered what a lot there is to like about him.

There are times when the relationship between the person being supported and a member of their team is so good that we would never consider moving the member of staff. Support worker Gilda has a wonderful relationship with Alice based on a mutual, cheeky sense of humour and a well-developed sense of the ridiculous. They have a lovely time together and are a great match. Gari has a fantastic relationship with Justin and is amazingly charismatic and confident. This calmness and charisma works perfectly for Justin as it enables him to feel perfectly safe so they can just have a nice time together. Gari's insightfulness is a great help when the team are struggling to understand what is happening for Justin; often Gari works it out while the rest of us are still scratching our heads. Yvonne sees Catherine as a strong, determined person and admires her; this has helped Catherine to feel respected and has cemented their relationship which has now become a friendship.

Rebecca

We always think carefully about what someone needs before we choose the staff team. When we started to support Rebecca we knew that her team manager needed to be able to support someone with high levels of anxiety, who would be unwavering even in times of challenge and very calm and relaxed. Agnes had been working in Justin's team as a support worker and had done a great job. She'd learnt lots about working with someone with high levels of anxiety and had an amazing inner calm. Agnes was appointed the team manager for Rebecca's team and has been excellent at helping Rebecca to settle into her new home. Agnes has been able to support both the new team and Rebecca to get used to each other very quickly and Rebecca loves her new life. Agnes's unwavering belief in Rebecca has been very important.

Our ethos dictates that we appoint team managers from within Getta Life. This is important because it means we can be sure that the person's values are in accord with our own and, because we know them, we can be more confident in assigning the right team manager to the right person. This gives a career structure for the support workers too which is very positive and encouraging for them. Sometimes we have support staff who only ever work with one person in their time with Getta Life; this is because they start in the right place. Morris was a support worker in Matthew's team when we started supporting Matthew; he is now the team manager. Because Morris has been on the journey with Matthew he can help new members of the team to understand his story very quickly, and for Matthew it's great to have been supported by the same person for a good number of years. It's easy for Matthew to trust Morris and to feel confident in his support.

There are times when it's clear that relationships aren't working. When this happens we try to help the support worker to change their approach and to consider how they can improve the relationship. Sometimes this works and people can continue working together. An example of this is when Simon started to work with Patrick. Initially he wasn't very good at listening either to Patrick or his Getta Life colleagues; we discussed this with him in supervision, and in team meetings we talked about the importance of listening. Simon acknowledged he was struggling with something in his personal life and that this was affecting his work. Shortly after this there was an improvement in Simon's listening and now he's really in tune with Patrick and Patrick is really comfortable with Simon. Last year they went on holiday together and this cemented their relationship and deepened their understanding of each other. Now Simon talks movingly about moments he has with Patrick where he feels they've really connected. These days, he's insightful about Patrick; if Patrick is unhappy Simon will often have a good idea why. Recently Patrick got very anxious and unable to settle in the daytime; he wasn't able to wait for things and would become very cross when things he wanted weren't instantly granted. Patrick wasn't sleeping well and generally was much more anxious than he had been for some time. Simon talked to us about the point when Patrick got distressed; it had followed him having a lovely time with Minnie when she'd visited his home. Immediately after Minnie left, Patrick became agitated and continued to be very unhappy for two weeks. We talked to Patrick and Minnie about what had happened and we asked Minnie whether Patrick could see her each week so that it could become a regular part of his life. We hoped this would help him to cope with saying goodbye to her, knowing he would get to spend some time with her each week. After two weeks Patrick settled again and is seeing Minnie regularly. Without Simon's insight we might have missed this possibility as we know Patrick often has periods of not sleeping.

Often we can tell from how the supported person is when they're with their staff member whether or not the relationship is working. The people we support are very good at showing us when they aren't happy with the person supporting them and if the support worker can't make it right we think carefully about where they might be better placed. This is always a difficult decision as it means disrupting someone else's team, so we do this with lots of thought and consideration.

Jane (not her real name) worked in Justin's team and we had to move her to work in another team as she got very frightened after an incident with Justin. She was often very critical of her colleagues and also struggled not to let her own life issues impact on Justin's life. Shortly after moving to another team she left Getta Life as she found the levels of relationship required too difficult for her.

Valerie (not her real name) was quite new to Getta Life and came to work in Minnie's team. It quickly became apparent that it wouldn't work because Valerie couldn't understand or accept that Minnie couldn't help the way she behaved, that this was part of Minnie's mental health issues and that it wasn't acceptable to describe Minnie's way of behaving in a way that blamed. Valerie moved to another team where she did a little better but again she left quite quickly as she struggled with the level of commitment required to do the work well. Sometimes people don't have enough energy to be in a good relationship at work. It's reassuring to us, reflecting on this issue as we write this chapter, to see that anyone who isn't getting the relationship right is given help to change, and if they can't they leave. The Getta Life ethos of relationships is so strong that people can't stay working within the organisation if they aren't able to be in a good relationship with the person they support.

Levels of relationships, heartfulness and deep connections

To be in a good relationship with others you must first be able to be in a good relationship with yourself, open to reflection and considering change. It's probably helpful if you're good at relationships or at least comfortable about being in relationships with people. People's needs are best served by people whose own needs are well met. This might seem like a trite statement and trips easily off the tongue but what kind of person does it actually reflect? I guess it means people who are well-rounded, kind and insightful and who can put someone else's needs before their own. This doesn't mean that people can't expect to be considered in the relationship, but it does mean that they can't expect the person they support to fill their gaps for them. If your own needs are well met you are much more likely to tune into someone else and respond to their needs. If you're struggling with your own needs you are more likely to misinterpret things and make the wrong decisions.

Karl
Karl has moved house while we've been supporting him. He was able to buy his home using a shared ownership scheme, which meant he could choose exactly where to live. He looked at lots of different properties, and the one he bought was where he immediately felt comfortable and settled when he looked round. He smiled lots, was very calm and not anxious at all. On moving day Karl coped very well with the move; we had been worried that he might find it disturbing and become anxious again. We'd gone to a lot of effort to make sure all of

Karl's photos and pictures were up in his new home and that his furniture was all set up by the end of moving day. Karl surprised us because he managed the move in his usual style; he took the whole thing completely in his stride. Sadly his new neighbours did not. They struggled to welcome him into their street and got very concerned about his presence. There followed a number of complaints about various things; Karl's style of communication, how the team parked their cars, the value of their properties and numerous other things. Some of these complaints were written and we replied where we could; some were made anonymously. We had lots of conversations about how to support Karl well and how to help him be a good neighbour. Sadly some of our best ideas were disastrous in terms of Karl's PR. The team thought it would be helpful if the neighbours got used to seeing Karl so they might start to see him as a person. They thought that on Saturday mornings they would support Karl to wash his car. As Karl can't do this himself their plan was to wash the car while Karl played with his hula hoop and listened to music. As Karl is usually settled during this time we hoped that the neighbours would start to see Karl as a normal man on the block, maybe like the look of him and possibly be curious enough to want to get to know him more. But in fact this became one more thing they got cross about. One Saturday while Douglas, the team manager, was washing the car the situation escalated and ended up with Karl's neighbour shouting and swearing at him. It felt as though the situation had become unsafe and we didn't want the team to feel threatened while they were at work.

We decided to speak to the police who were very supportive; they visited the neighbour and facilitated a meeting between us and Karl's neighbours. They were very good at making sure everyone got heard; we were able to tell some of Karl's story and his neighbours were able to raise their concerns. This meeting was very difficult and uncomfortable but led to a much easier relationship for Karl. Karl's neighbours speak to both him and all of his support team now and there haven't been any further complaints. Karl received several Christmas cards from his neighbours last year which felt very positive. It was important in our commitment to Karl to be steadfast in our support; first of his right to live peacefully in his own home and second in our belief in his being a worthwhile person to be in a relationship with his neighbours. This kept us on track working for a solution rather than retreating into entrenched defensive mode.

CHAPTER 2
Relationships

KEY MESSAGES

- ☑ We all have a universal need to be loved and liked.
- ☑ The importance of trust.
- ☑ Work from the heart with love.
- ☑ Recognise that relationships take time, effort and thoughtfulness.
- ☑ Recognise the importance of relationships with families.
- ☑ Develop awareness that everyone wants relationships in their lives and follow the clues and possibilities.
- ☑ The relationship between the person being supported and their support worker must be the right relationship, they must like each other and it must be real.
- ☑ There is a natural solidarity with people when you are in a positive relationship with them.
- ☑ If things go wrong it's important not to lose faith in relationships.
- ☑ Recognise that people need time alone when they have twenty-four hour support.
- ☑ Be aware of people's previous experiences of relationships and the impact of these now.
- ☑ Everything the supported person does is communication and we need to be tuned in with that and learn the individual's language to be in a good relationship.
- ☑ Being yourself and being true to yourself is part of the work.

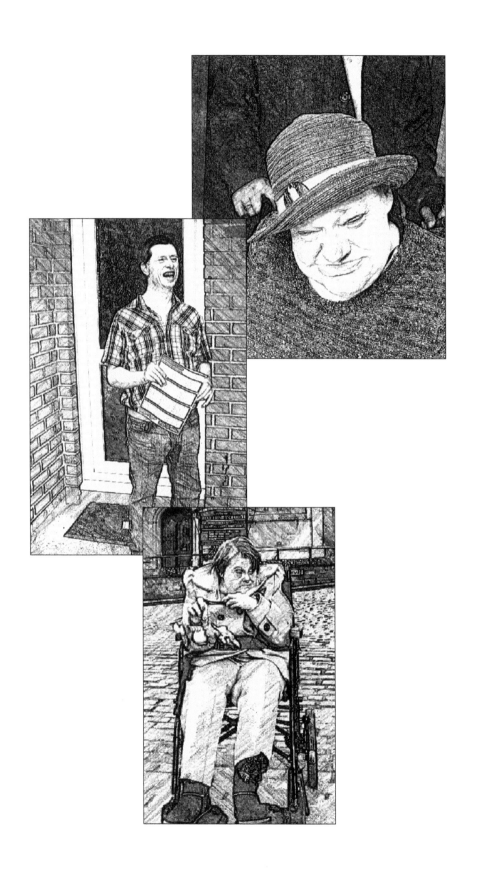

Chapter 3

From There to Here – Real Lives

Written by two mothers and Sue Deeley

Daniel's mum's story, in her own words

Daniel's life before he moved into Getta Life

When Daniel was born and I found out he was handicapped it was obviously a shock. It's a long time ago and in those days there wasn't really any help; that was it. Daniel was born at home as I wanted a home birth and looking back even the midwife didn't say to me, *'You have a handicapped child'*. Nothing was said to me; obviously I could see by his face that he was different. I had my second baby only fourteen months later with a different midwife; Daniel still couldn't walk or talk, he just made noises. This midwife said I should get some help with him and see what could be done; it was only then that I thought, *'Yes, I've got to do this'*.

Home was an upstairs maisonette, so life was quite difficult. It wasn't until Daniel was five years old that I started to get a bit of time during the day. He began to go out to school between ten o'clock and four o'clock; this continued until he was nine years old. During this time, I'd had another child, and we were still living in the maisonette, so things were very, very difficult. Daniel started to walk when he was about six years old and up until then I had to carry him everywhere, and this was quite stressful.

Eventually I had to agree that it would be better for the family – not for Daniel, but for the family – that he went away to a hospital. It was called Lea Castle Hospital or The Hospital. He was there for nine years, and we used to visit him every Sunday. There wasn't very much happening at the hospital; it's horrible to call it a hospital. There was a very, very large room with small bedrooms coming off it. If you took him toys they were taken away. I never saw them playing with toys of any description: they were all kept on a shelf in a small room. In the large room, there were tables and chairs, and outside there were fields and plenty of grass. Daniel loved being outside which was great in the summer, we used to have picnics. But whenever I took him back I used to have to call the nurses to unlock the door to this big room, and he would run in and get under the table which is where he would spend all his time. It was just heartbreaking to see him and other children there. There were some awful sights; nurses would wheel people around in big old-fashioned prams. Some of them had just a head and a body, no legs, no arms and with a beard on their face showing their age; they were living like that. There were many pitiful sights, it was terrible.

Daniel moved from Lea Castle Hospital to Harnell Lane in Coventry, where twelve to fifteen people lived. The government had decided to close such institutions as the hospitals, trying to get the patients into a home life by moving them into smaller houses or homes. Harnell Lane did try; it was the beginning of things, it was different from a hospital and I was able to see him more often. This was the start of the changes in Daniel's life.

Harnell Lane was two houses knocked into one, and there was still the same idea of everyone sitting around the edges, but they were able to go from room to room, it was more of a home. I noticed that Daniel would go and sit beside one of the other people there, Angela, and she with him; they always seemed to be together which was nice because it was the first time I had ever seen him actually being with someone instead of either hiding underneath the table or going off on his own somewhere. The people who ran the home also said they were always together.

I can't honestly remember how long he lived at Harnell Lane; maybe a year, maybe a little bit longer. Then the community nurse who dealt with people like Daniel and Angela in Coventry mentioned them to Sue and Julie, who were starting up Getta Life. They went to see Daniel and Angela and then Sue got in touch with me and told me about Getta Life and this whole new idea of theirs.

At first I admit I thought, he seems to be OK where he is, and I didn't like the name Getta Life to be honest!

The move to Getta Life
I did meet Sue and was very taken with her; she explained this lovely, lovely idea of trying to get people into their own homes. Eventually it happened, and it's been absolutely brilliant from then on. I honestly can't praise Getta Life enough, not just Sue and Julie, but everyone who works there, not just in Daniel's and Angela's home, but in all of them, they're brilliant. Everyone is so friendly; it's like a big family and we all meet up occasionally.

Daniel's life now
Somehow Getta Life comes up with ideas for everyone. At one time, Daniel would go to a centre and then go back home later in the afternoon. At the centre all he would really do was sit there, they were able to play with things but I think he didn't really want to join in. But it's changed; now they take him to college, he's learning to cook and to prepare things. He goes

carriage riding, and he absolutely loves horses. They're going sailing and there's a men's night. Robert, one of his support workers, introduced him to swimming and got him a season ticket for the rugby, it used to be football but I didn't like it, so they changed it to rugby. He takes Daniel on a train, he introduces him to the public; they go shopping together, and they are known in their neighbourhood.

Angela does different things on different days; she goes to knitting classes and a women's group and sometimes they go to the pub together. They do the things normal people do, they're not shut away because they can't speak or express themselves as others do. They have a lovely life, they really do.

Getta Life has given them a chance to have a taste of life. It's as though Getta Life has a huge pair of arms and they've got everyone in a circle and they're looking after them all, they're all cocooned and safe. They are showing them that you can do lovely things even though you can't walk or talk, you can still enjoy your life, and they are getting a life.

My thoughts and feelings

I can see how happy Daniel is, but when you give birth to a child such as Daniel, you think why, what have I done wrong, and in a way I felt ashamed. I knew of one neighbour who had a disabled child, not as handicapped as Daniel, and they kept him at home until he died in his twenties. I feel ashamed that I couldn't do that. I know I'm human, and I've got my faults as well and just because I'm a mother I can't do everything; you think you can, but you can't. I'm just not strong enough in a sense.

I am spiritual, and I used to pray, especially when Daniel was in Lea Hospital and I could see other people far worse than him. I would ask God, 'Why do you allow this sort of thing to happen?' and 'Why are you creating people like this?' A few years ago I started to attend a spiritual church. I believe in God and that we are all here with a purpose and I definitely believe there is an afterlife… He is a brilliant son; I'm his mother, and I'm proud of him.

Collin's story, told by his mum

Collin went into the care system very young, eventually moving into a hospital when he was fourteen. When Collin reached his fortieth birthday at Christmas in 2012, he had been living in his own home, supported by Getta Life, for three months. By the time he moved he had lived at the hospital for nearly twenty-six years and hadn't been out of the grounds for well over fourteen.

Life has been quite a challenge for him, but he's been really good and I'm very proud of him. Moving into his own home has been like switching a radio on – it's like he's been brought back to life.

Collin's life before moving into his own home
Collin was nearly 10lb when he was born and I kept going to the doctor to ask for help as I couldn't get him to take the bottle. When he was ten months old he was really poorly and the doctor tried to say it was my fault as I wasn't feeding him properly. In the end I found out that if I massaged his neck as I fed him it helped the food go down; it was as if I was teaching him how to eat. The doctor didn't offer any help and I know they would have blamed me if he had died. I nearly lost him; it was one of the scariest things.

When Collin was about nine months old I took him to an assessment centre and he stayed there until he started special school at two. Up until then they wouldn't tell me anything, they just said he needed looking after. When they decided he could go to school they said, '*Well of course he'll be going to a special school because he is mentally handicapped,*' and that was the first time I knew.

He went to school until he was five and then he went to boarding school. At first they were really positive with him and then when he got to thirteen or fourteen years old he was sometimes violent and they seemed to lose interest in him because of this. In the end they got him into a local hospital, which was an old mental hospital.

The people at the hospital didn't bother to find him another school but they had a swimming pool they used to hire out to other special schools. Someone from one of the schools who used the pool saw Collin and wanted to know why he wasn't in school. He was lucky as they took him in until he was nineteen. He still lived at the hospital but went to the school every day; it was in the country down a quiet lane and he did lots of walking. They wanted to keep him on but they couldn't as he was too old. So he just stayed in hospital.

He was quite happy until the late 1990s when he was taken shopping at a big supermarket; something scared him, I'm not sure what, and he lost his temper. I don't know all the details as I found out from other people not the hospital. I can't really blame the shop as they were looking after their shoppers but their security guards got involved and I think made it worse. It eventually took eight of them to get him out of the store.

As a result of this Collin was scared and became isolated. At first the staff said he was refusing to go out; he only went into the back garden. He wouldn't go beyond the hospital and they kept blaming the incident in the supermarket. Gradually the staff stopped asking him and then they wouldn't take him out.

When he was younger he was very social and he would wander around the hospital grounds. I'm not sure if the supermarket incident was completely to blame as unfortunately they sold off a lot of the hospital and built a housing estate. Collin used to be able to go for walks, knock on doors and ask for a cup of tea at whatever ward he decided to visit. They would make him a cup of tea and give him some biscuits and then send him back to his own ward. When the houses were built the people got fed up with him knocking on their doors. He wasn't the only person living at the hospital doing this so the hospital had to start locking the ward doors; they had to start locking the patients in. He did change quite a lot when the housing estate was built and a friend of mine said that if he had been born normal they would probably have diagnosed him with depression.

For his last ten years at the hospital he was living in the property on his own. It was like a large house with a very large garden. The property itself was OK but they changed the staff every three to four hours, so no one worked with Collin for more than four hours at a time.

Quite a few of the staff were OK, although the younger ones were a bit quiet. I used to visit once a month but they didn't make you feel very welcome, it was hard. When I used to visit he would ask to go for a walk. There was a WRVS shop so we used to spend most of our time together there. On his birthday once, which is in December, I went to visit him on the ward and none of his birthday cards were up. When I asked them where they were they said, '*It's not Christmas yet*'. I said, '*No, I brought his birthday cards over, not his Christmas ones.*' They had just put them away.

When he was younger he used to talk and he had quite a good sense of humour. If we ever had visitors he would go round the room looking at them and he would suddenly sit and look in a certain direction and once he'd got their attention and they looked at where he was looking he used to take their cakes. He was quite a character and you can gradually see it coming back.

Towards the end of his time at the hospital he was just staying in the house. He was being given his tea around 5 or 6 p.m., then he would be given his tablets and he'd be in bed before 7 p.m.

If I think back to the 1970s I feel hurt and bewildered. Rather than offering me the help I needed, like today, they were looking for a reason for Collin's difficulties and it had to be the parents' fault. It was quite scary although I didn't realise it at the time. Looking back now at the way people in the 1970s viewed it, it's quite horrific. The fact is if he had died I don't know what would have happened to me.

Why Collin moved

I felt quite let down by the hospital. They said they were going to support Collin during his transition period between his life at the hospital and being supported by Getta Life and moving to his new home in Coventry. The hospital said they would work alongside Sue and Sophie from Getta Life and gradually pull back from Collin by going into another room while he got used to Sue and Sophie. Then they would do a similar thing when he moved into his new home in Coventry. But actually as soon as he made the move they said they couldn't let the staff come because they weren't insured. They were concerned that Collin would lose his temper, so when Getta Life really needed their support they refused to give it. And when Getta Life got involved, the hospital suddenly started taking him out after they'd stopped offering him the opportunity of outings a long time ago; for instance they took him to Weston Super Mare. They said their reasoning for this sudden change was he needed to get used to going out otherwise he wouldn't be able to move to Coventry, but you can't help but wonder why they didn't take him out before.

I know they gave him a bad reputation at the hospital. They wouldn't call his new bungalow home when he went to visit because they thought if he called it home he'd get confused and kick up a temper tantrum, so they just used to call it the bungalow, and because of this Collin still calls it the bungalow, not home.

It made me quite angry: the reason he was moving was because they were going to close all the big hospitals down. After he'd moved they said there was going to be an investigation into why Collin had been left there for so long without anyone trying to do anything. I looked at them and asked them what they had to say; they said, *'You do realise this will never happen again,'* and I said, *'Well you're closing it down so it won't happen again.'* I don't think they will look into it now; they'll forget about it. I'm not talking so much about the support staff, although some felt more like control staff than support, but the people higher up; they aren't going to bother now he's gone. Collin's been in his new home a year and I haven't heard anything except one phone call from the hospital asking him how he was getting on about six months after he moved; it was nice to get the call.

Moving on

We had been looking for somewhere for Collin to move to for ten years and I was told that he should be staying in Birmingham but they couldn't find anywhere. Then a lady talked about Getta Life and said she'd have a word with Sue to see if she would talk to me. I met Sue once at the hospital and then she came to my house and left some DVDs about what they had accomplished with other service users they look after. She said as she was leaving that Collin would definitely be getting out in the future, once they'd moved him into the bungalow at Coventry. She said it might take a long time because of how long he's been refusing to go out. The week Collin moved, Sue phoned up towards the end of the week and she said, *'I thought we'd let you know that he's amazing and we can't believe how many times he's been out, in fact he asked to go out the day after moving in.'* She said, *'You should be so proud of him.'* I put the phone down and I cried. It's like having him back, I didn't realise how much he had gone into himself until he started coming out of himself.

The differences since moving

I noticed straight away before I'd even visited him that things were different. The three people who supported him kept phoning me up and telling me what Collin had been doing; when they rang I could hear him in the background telling them what to say to me. Nobody did that for him before, yet it's such a little thing.

I know this is only small but I went to see him a couple of months ago and we were sitting out in the garden and he asked me to come and sit on the same bench as him. It's the first time he's ever asked me to do anything like that. His life has changed about one hundred per cent.

My older daughter spends time with him now since he's moved; she didn't like the hospital. I have a photo in my house of Collin, my daughter, my other son and his girlfriend; it's lovely seeing a family together like that.

I think it's incredible. I've watched this past year and been really amazed at what he's been doing, things I didn't think he ever would. He looks up more when you're talking, he used to walk around looking at the ground; the people at the hospital always said it was because his sight isn't very good. He talks about things that happened when he was a child so he's getting lots more vocal. I am really amazed and really proud of him, I can't believe how somebody who has had the type of life that he has is able to flourish like he is; it's incredible.

How I'm supported now
I think the big thing for me, and I didn't expect it and I really couldn't expect it, was that I thought it was going to be difficult to get to see Collin, but Sue said, *'We'll come and fetch you and take you to the bungalow any time you want to come and see him.'* It started off as twice a month and now it's usually once a month but that's because of the shifts I do.

It takes about an hour, sometimes more, from Collin's bungalow to my house. When Collin first moved they weren't sure if he would do the journey to my house with them because you have to come into the area near the hospital. So at first Sophie would fetch me and take me to see him. She would do a whole day at work and just come and pick me up with Collin and then bring me back with them. Now he just comes to pick me up with whoever is on shift and he did that within three to four visits, so a couple of months from moving in.

Getta Life support me a lot. I have to go into hospital this month, only day surgery but Sophie phoned me up and said, 'Can we bring Collin into see you at the hospital?' I think I will probably be out by the time they get there but it was lovely that she offered.

What I would tell other people whose children need support
I would definitely put Getta Life forward as people to go and see. I can't believe how Collin has changed. I know that Getta Life staff are trained for two weeks before they start to work with somebody, because I was asked to join in. I just think

that their whole outlook is amazing. They are so positive. I didn't think it could go so smoothly after the length of time that he had spent in hospital.

Collin's story – a move to a brighter future

Written by Sue Deeley of Getta Life

Reputations can damage people's lives in the present and in the future. The extent to which this can impact on people is still able to shock me. Collin had lived in healthcare settings for the past twenty years, mainly in a long-stay hospital for people with learning difficulties. Most recently he lived alone with an ever-changing rota of staff supporting him from another ward. This followed a difficult episode in a supermarket and a catastrophic period of illness. Collin lost his freedom and most of his young adult life because people didn't know what else to do.

The people around him were frightened that he would hurt himself and believed he could only be supported in an institutional setting, deeming he needed special solitary, sound-proofed accommodation because of his autism. He had experienced a lot of physical intervention, mechanical restraining, high levels of medication and ECT. I believe people only use these approaches when they don't know what else to do; there is no doubt that everyone was stuck. How could people know what else to do when they were working in a setting that had invested so much in the building of his reputation?

When asked whether we, Getta Life, could support him to try and live in the community again we agreed to give it a go. We were told that he would need night staff and two people with him at all times while in the community, I suppose to replicate the hospital. Perhaps the most restrictive label that Collin had was that he must not be over-stimulated. The staff believed he had specific sensory processing difficulties and there was a risk he may become unwell if this was permitted. I think this severely limited his life and allowed the staff to hide behind the fear and not actively engage with Collin. This resulted in him living an empty life for many years. Imagine for yourself what impact that label would have on you? My guess is that it would probably end up denying you most of the things that added value and interest to your life. How would it be to live with that label because the people supposed to be supporting you didn't know what to do if you got excited?

There was a lot of fear about the risk this move presented to Collin but little thought was given to the risk posed by his staying in hospital. When we met Collin and started to get to know him, what we learnt didn't match the reputation. We met someone who is perceptive, clever, warm, friendly, interesting, fascinating and fun. We were told he couldn't be informed that he was moving as this would disturb him. The last time he had moved was within the hospital setting when he'd been told he was going for a walk. He was actually being moved to another ward and he wouldn't be going back – but he wasn't told that. He was given no explanation nor any opportunity to say goodbye to what in effect had become his home; he simply never returned. No wonder he reacted badly.

Supporting Collin in his move
Initially Sophie, the team manager we appointed to support Collin and his new team, spent time with him, gradually building up the time she spent alone with him. It was clear he enjoyed talking to her, and Sophie discovered that he liked gardening and getting involved in preparing food, and that he showed an interest in the world. Once Sophie and Collin's relationship was becoming established two new support staff were introduced and they started to work with him, still on the hospital site. Gradually they were left to work alone with him so they could start to build relationships with each other.

We found him a bungalow in Coventry, importantly one with a big garden that we thought would suit him and give him space. We invited his mum to come and take a look and get her opinion; she loved it.

Then when we had permission we started to help Collin visit Coventry, popping into the bungalow for cups of tea, gradually building up the time he spent away from his ward. Sophie painted pictures of bungalows and asked Collin what he would like to put in his new home. We bought an iPad which Collin used to show us the furniture he liked. We also took Collin to a garage to choose his car, a red car. We arranged for the garage to bring the car to the local park where Collin went walking so he could be taken in the car for a test drive. The car was delivered a few days before Collin moved into his new home.

The move
On moving day, Collin got to his bungalow and said, 'The old ward's closed now, it's burnt down!!' Collin showed us he had worked out he had moved. After a few weeks he showed us the many things he can do; he helps to look after his home and has quickly learnt his way around although he only sees a little. He enjoys being in the kitchen and has a chair right next to the cooker. He loves taking a long walk every morning and in fact he told Sophie, '*My legs are better now.*' Collin's mum visits and he goes with her in his new car when she's taken home. Collin showed us he is ready for life again; how long has he been ready, I wonder?

In his first team meeting we were reflecting on what had gone well in first month. Collin said, '*It's better now!*' That says it all.

A year on
It is now over a year since Collin moved into his new home. During this time Collin's team have developed good, close relationships with him. The same three people still love working with him. Collin has loved re-connecting with his family and has enjoyed having his mum, grandad and sister to visit in his home. They are all delighted to see the Collin they know and remember slowly reappearing. Collin skypes his mum and speaks to his family and team on the phone when he wants

to; this reassures him that even if they're not with him they still care for him.

He does his shopping locally; at the greengrocers he visits every week Theresa and Tazz talk to him, the staff at the building society know Collin by name and chat to him. His neighbours know him and look out for him when he is walking by. The security guard at the Co-op gave Sophie some unsolicited feedback; he told her that he was really impressed with how well the team support Collin and that he couldn't fault any of it! How much safer is Collin now with the security guard in the Co-op watching and noticing how he is supported in contrast to his not being seen by anyone except staff in the hospital setting?

Collin is talking much more readily and clearly; he is healthy and very fit. A recent assessment by an occupational therapist found that Collin's sensory needs are being met by his current lifestyle; his home and his range of activities meet them perfectly.

I believe this is because his support team know him well, follow his lead and respond to his feedback. Collin tells us when he has had enough; we respect that and respond to it while gently encouraging him to try new things. A visitor who knew him in the hospital says he looks fifteen years younger.

Final thoughts

We must seriously re-think assessment and treatment settings and their part in enhancing people's negative reputations. I believe they directly contribute to people's distress, isolation and loneliness. We must learn to try things even when we don't know the way or whether things will work out. If we don't, how many more lives will get wasted, lost in a system that is paralysed through not knowing how to help? As with Collin, how long have other people been ready for life?

CHAPTER 3
From There to Here – Real Lives

KEY MESSAGES

- ☑ Acknowledge that it's a real ask to expect parents and families to trust new providers as some people with learning difficulties have been treated badly by the care provision system.

- ☑ We must seriously re-think assessment and treatment settings and their part in enhancing people's negative reputations.

- ☑ Try new things even when you don't know what the outcome will be.

- ☑ Do everything you can to prevent people getting lost in a system that doesn't know how to help them.

- ☑ Be aware that there are still people being made to live in institutionalised type environments.

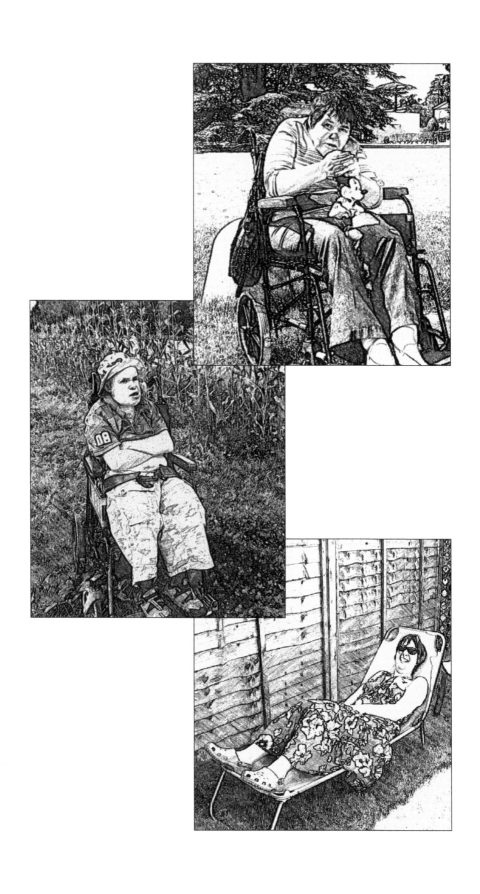

Chapter 4

How Circles and Teams Reflect the Person

Written by Andy Smith of Diversity Matters

Most of us are lucky enough to have people in our life who naturally support us. For many, these people are our family, for others it is a circle of friends who help us share our joy and generally live life, keeping in touch and offering support where necessary. Most of us have a mixture of family and friends who go through life alongside us.

Some people with learning difficulties have lost touch with their families, have been rejected by them or are the only surviving family member. They may have few friends and can be very lonely or isolated. There are many people with learning difficulties for whom the only people in their lives are those who are paid to be there: a support team. This chapter talks about how to continually ensure the support team is a good fit and works to support the person in making friendships.

This chapter also describes how to help develop circles of support for those people who don't have meaningful friendships in their life. The purpose of a circle is to add meaning to someone's life by showing them they matter. Circles protect people, both because there are outsiders looking in and because it helps to give the person a sense of worth. This in turn develops the person's self-esteem, which builds resilience and makes them less vulnerable.

Circles in practice

I have always loved curries, but since visiting Sarah my taste has changed and remarkably so. I have learnt that there are curries and then there are the curries that Sarah's support worker, Promila, makes with her. Everyone who has tasted one remembers it with a smile. And on this bright spring morning as I visit Sarah at home, a wonderful smell percolates, escaping the open kitchen window, while Sarah, supported by Promila, prepares food for lunch.

This will not be an ordinary lunchtime. Today, Sarah's circle is meeting at her house. Around 12.30pm people begin to arrive, shouting their hellos, greeting Sarah and each other with real pleasure, like old friends coming together. Many bring gifts or perhaps a card to thank or appreciate her for something and by 1.00pm the room is full. People chat, eat and drink. Others read to Sarah or reminisce about good times they had together and dream about the future.

Marjorie, a retired public servant, is one of Sarah's circle members and she talks about her delight at being in Sarah's circle and the gratitude she feels about being invited in:

> *'We are men and women of different ages so we all have something different to bring to Sarah. For some reason we are a supportive and engaging group—perhaps more so because Sarah hasn't had much opportunity in her life to express herself.'*

And here I think Marjorie captured something about the essence of Sarah's circle. It's an engaged and lively group that is good in itself but one which also creates the right conditions so that Sarah can be herself and express herself as she really is.

> *'The group is creative and embraces different ways of thinking. We are very proud of Sarah's progress and how she has changed, and also how some of the staff who work with her have changed too.'*

So, why do Sarah and others like her need this circle of support? What are these alliances or clusters of folk trying to achieve? To understand this we have to remember and look hard at many of the common life experiences of people with learning difficulties. It is easy to turn a blind eye to these common experiences because they are (and should be) a cause for national and international shame. We know for example that many people have experienced sudden and unexpected separation from their communities, families and friends, supposedly in order that they get help! People have been removed and taken to institutions (and still suffer this in many countries), and the majority will have been moved around for the sake of the administration's efficiency drives or for institutional needs. And through this process, people often end up alone, with few if any friends, and sadly without the ordinary and simple relationships that the rest of us take for granted. Relationships where one feels belonging, trust, camaraderie, acceptance and love are often missing and for some may never have been present.

So when people who have had these negative life experiences first meet an organisation that works more humanely and is rooted in the ordinary community they unsurprisingly have difficulties understanding ordinary relationships. They may be more skilled at spotting distrust rather than trust, more able to spot a lie than the truth. Also, they may (though not always) need help to reconnect with family and in some cases be unable to even recognise ordinary family life, friendship or neighbourliness. This means organisations have to pay constant attention to fundamental questions such as who the new key people are in a supported person's life, how can they be introduced, and how can people from the past be re-introduced too.

Later in this chapter we will look at some of the ways it is possible to arrange the team of workers around the person so that the relationships are right for all. We will also look at how to organise 'circles of support' or 'circles of friends'. Both these ideas require the creation of a mini community focused on settling the person into ordinary life. There are different ways to solve these problems and each supported person is a unique starting point.

As another circle member says, *'Sarah can't speak to you directly and tell you about her life, but being part of the circle you kind of link in with her and get a real sense of what a good life is all about for her. I can connect with her life and get a sense of what it's all about. Now I know she is a kindred spirit, it isn't any kind of chore – it's a lovely home to go to where I can pop in. It's great to visit, it's a privilege.'*

One way to begin is to discover the right match

Try and imagine that for the next few years you're going to spend the majority of your time, week in and week out, with the same small group of people. You haven't met them yet, but you know that they're going to be in your personal space every day (big time), perhaps helping you eat, perhaps helping you bathe and use the toilet. They will be present when you're with friends and acquaintances, and they will be nearby when you want to be alone. This small group will always be with you in some way or another. How would you choose them? What qualities would you need them to have? How likely do you think it will be that you'll make the correct decision straight off and choose the perfect team at the first attempt?

It's a serious business, this matching of team members with the person to be supported. Like any matching process, if you get it wrong a lot of unhappiness may result. Get it right and life won't only be much easier for you, it will be a breeze.

So any organisation intending to do this kind of work well needs to apply maximum effort to one of the oldest human questions: *what has to happen so that people get along with other people?* It's maybe the most crucial part of the job, and getting these relationships right depends partly on having a sense of what being with the other person is really about. Everyone is different of course and each person within each team or circle of relationships should reflect these differences.

Jonathan and Zara are a brother and sister who live together and for their needs to be well met, a group of people who can help them feel safe is pivotal. The team members they have around them now are consistent, gentle and steady, a combination that has led over time to Jonathan and Zara opening up and revealing their hidden skills and personalities. A different example is Peter, who requires a team that is relaxed about touch, and for whom being on the move is the norm. Alice's team is different again; being quirky and independent-minded, the members reflect Alice's ways and ensure her personality is developed and valued.

It may sound simple but having a good basic idea of the essence of the person and their main concerns can help in getting the right team around them. This means figuring out some central themes that need to be right for the person in terms of where they are today and the person they are growing to become.

Karl's sister told us about the workers he has in his team:

> *'They have a very important approach to being with Karl in that they keep out of the way when Karl comes to stay or visit with us. They don't interfere, they're discreet and stay in the background – it's more like they're hanging out together with him rather than being his staff – they create a warm and accepting atmosphere.'*

It's not by accident that the team members are like this. They've first of all learnt to facilitate different situations when they're with Karl and to act uniquely with him so he can enjoy the company of each individual he's with. They pay attention and try to create the right atmosphere, environment and way of being with Karl that really works for him. This approach reflects how they are within themselves. Therapists and counsellors refer to these inner skills as congruence and authenticity. Workers who are able to self-reflect and consider how their own mood and attitude are part of the process for Karl and take responsibility for their internal world and its reactions end up being the most successful workers for him.

Claire's team provides us with a similar example. This is a team that is complex and fun, where members think hard about how life is for Claire and work to understand her and support her in sensitive ways. It's a team that reflects Claire's personality and needs, so members are often happy to drop what they're doing to play, dance, sing or take that spirit into their work as they spend time with her. Felicity, Claire's sister, reflects on how being in Claire's team could be a 24/7 intense and personal experience:

> *'You have to like her if you work with her and she has to like you – there is no other way for it to work. Recruiting the team is about understanding people's characters and how they might fit.'*

Felicity, as Claire's sister, was involved in recruiting the team, sitting in on interviews and helping in induction, and this insight is also of significant importance. Some organisations often try and get the perfect job description in an effort to define the ideal team member, when in fact it can boil down to something more mysterious and magical. Perhaps it will be an eternal mystery; after all, poets and artists as well as psychologists are still trying to figure out exactly why some relationships click and work well when others do not. The bottom line though must be as Claire's sister says:

> *'...You have to like her and she you – there is no other way – the team are not family but sometimes it feels like that.'*

Having said all this, the matching and initial recruitment is only one milestone on the road to success and it's also what happens afterwards that makes the difference.

The more tuned-in the team is to the person, the better the support will be

---

Over the years, we've realised that the qualities we find amongst the best teams seem to evolve naturally to closely match the needs of the person they're supporting. Like every developing process it's one that needs time, and although it initially appears as a natural process, on reflection we've realised that it's often nurtured and strengthened by great supervision and management support. Other factors are helpful too, for instance having a deliberate and carefully thought-through development strategy for the team. This needs to make enough time available so that team members can spend fruitful periods thinking about how to get it right for the person they are supporting. It helps if there's time spent in team meetings to think about and then go over the same topics with a focus on what's being learnt, with supervision meetings having the same focus. Workers also need to reflect on the qualities they're cultivating in themselves. And the organisation and managers need to give a clear and consistent message: you have to be in the right relationship with people to support them well. As teams get to know the person and work with them for some time, the role-modelling they can provide for newer staff following behind gets better and better.

We know from experience (so this is not just an unproven belief) that people are safer when supported by people with whom they have a relationship, as opposed to professionals who come in to 'care' and who are following only a care plan or protocol. People tend to be less safe when relationships are less deep or only last for a short period. In a way this is obvious common sense; folk don't take advantage of someone they genuinely care about, are committed to and who gives them something back.

How circles and teams work together
The involvement of the family or circle of support is needed as well as that of the support team. So for instance, looking back we can see that Neil's team has evolved in a particular way and with a set of particular qualities. Members are

attentive, detailed, thorough, careful and safe. To be like this is absolutely essential if his complex health needs are to be addressed properly, and if he's able to live life to the full when he's well, without anxiety about *'What if?'*. So complacency is pushed out and vigilance is built into the team's work. This has come about not just because of the organisation's work with the team but because of the concerns that are stressed to the team by Neil's circle of support.

Sarah's circle was highly influential in her health care and provides a great example of how teams and the circle can work together. When Sarah first became ill, the circle was very insistent about making sure she got the best treatment and the most thorough investigations so that her diagnosis was as accurate as possible. This isn't to say that the team wasn't also focused on getting the best health care, but the circle added another level of concern and the necessary weight to take on the unconscious prejudice in the health service around people with learning difficulties. (I don't mean to criticise individual health workers here but there is a lot of research that supports this statement; e.g. Eric Emerson and Susannah Baines: *Health Inequalities & People with Learning Disabilities in the UK: 2010 Learning Disabilities Observatory*.) So the circle adds something very important; a certain gravity, an insistence that's sometimes required to get things moving so that more thorough and careful investigations are made. Such things can be lifesaving. Asking the difficult questions, not taking '*No*' or '*Don't know*' for an answer is crucial when workers might not have the confidence or skills to do that on their own. It helps too for the team to know there is a circle of support in the background; having back-up when you need it.

How to involve the person in the team or circle
Team meetings evolve in ways that are good for the person whose team it is. For example, Claire's team meetings take place away from her home as she doesn't like it if we're all in her house at once: everyone usually goes to the pub! Patrick

frequently prefers to hold his in the car, sometimes it's parked but often the group talk while driving around. Karl likes to walk and play with his hula hoop during his meetings.

Rebecca's team meeting takes place in her lounge or her garden and always includes the manager bringing fruit or ice cream to eat. If and when Rebecca wants to leave she can, but she can listen in from other parts of the house, so she still gets to know what's happening while she's in a space that's most comfortable for her.

Charlie's circle meetings are called family teas. They are organised by his dad and all his family come for tea, giving them a chance to chat and catch up with each other. The team supports Charlie to prepare food and get in some drinks and often they help him to show his photos as a way of telling people what he has been doing.

Catherine's circle is focused quite differently and significantly on her family, who live in France. As a result she is supported so that she can have them come to stay with her and be the hostess or go abroad and visit them when she wants to.

Alice has both her sister and her best friend Wyn at the core of her circle and they like taking morning coffee and cakes with her. This is just the right balance for Alice as she doesn't like eating in wider company or welcoming more than a couple of visitors at a time.

Attachment

On my first day of work as a classroom assistant in a residential special school in 1980 I was told by an old hand at the job, *'Just make sure you don't get too close to the kids, son; it's not fair on you or them.'* This was not an unusual piece of advice then or now, but in my view it is fatally flawed. It's not that being closely attached is a required behaviour either, but given that so many people in the world are lonely and have few intimate relationships it seems utter madness not to get involved or close to some people you meet just because of a belief system or because of routines that exist in the service world. Every relationship and set of relationships is different and needs to be considered on its own terms. Supported people, team workers and circle members may all need help at some time to think about their relationships, but if they're not open to being close and letting something develop then little richness or depth results.

My second job in a support role was working within residential care with young people who had multiple labels and I was lucky to have a great mentor then who gave me some brilliant advice in the opposite direction: *'If you don't care deeply and also be yourself you'll be no good to anybody...'*

Contrast as well as similarity
Veronica spent long years in residential placements and special schools. This left her feeling lonely and, as her parents said, *'...sent her backwards, where she didn't develop, mature, learn or change.'* Lately, she has grown into leading her own life. Her parents talk about Kate who is a member of Veronica's team, *'Oh, she was extremely shy but not any longer because she's met Veronica.'* Kate had to support Veronica at amateur dramatics. *'Now they are there, side by side, and because they've met each other both their lives are richer.'* Workers who report they are happiest at work will often tell you that it feels like they're encouraged to be in a real relationship; although they are responsible and have jobs to do, *'It's not quite like going to a workplace.'*

Veronica is in her forties but one of her workers is eighteen. Veronica's mum reflects on how *'They have pillow fights together and gossip over cups of tea; she loves that.'*

Each of us is a complex mix of many parts and teams can be that way too

> *'You don't want all the same types of people around you – but it's been like that in other places I have seen; if you don't quite fit into the box you won't do very well with that organisation. But here it's all different because there isn't a box – there is a deeper listening to the depth of who people are.'* – A circle member talking about a staff team.

When any of us reflect on our own friendships and our family, work and leisure relationships we notice that we're not always the same moment by moment. We are different with different folk and we can experience our relationships as distinct separate things. So, from this perspective, having a team of clones would be strange indeed. A common refrain in support work is 'consistency', the idea that folk should all be treated the same. This might be a red herring in support work. Consistency is something that isn't attained in the real world; our friends and work colleagues all treat us differently and these differences can make our day. Another circle member said:

> *'It's great when supported people don't look like people in care – it's because of the focus Getta Life place on self-confidence and self-worth.'*

Knowing why you need a circle and what for!

Not everyone needs a circle. Rebecca's family has continued over the years to build and include her in networks of friends and family. So she is now well connected and known by a large number of people who can look out for her and who she can link in with if the need arises. In circumstances such as these the team's focus is on enabling relationships to grow. They are discreet, simply hanging out in the group with the supported person and their network and fitting in while providing exactly the right level of support.

Some things a circle can do

If a supported person doesn't have decent connections into family or community life or networks of people, or if he or she has spent much of his or her life away in institutions, then creating a circle can have some absolutely crucial benefits. On one level, circles are a great way to keep people safer. A circle acts as a safeguard because of four good reasons:

1. Everyone needs to know that they are known, looked out for and understood. If a person knows they're looked out for by others then they are more confident, because they know they can get help if they need it.

2. Circles help people because they send out clear messages to wider society that this person is of concern, importance and value to others, is appreciated and is being watched over.

3. Circles help the person discover themselves, enriching their self-esteem, self-knowledge and self-belief and confirming new identities for the person.

4. We all need a sense of belonging; a sense that we fit somewhere, with people like us and with whom we belong. The effects of not belonging anywhere have been well-documented and are not good.

Pat has been a member of Sarah's circle for a few years now. She is also the relative of a worker and was deliberately recruited into Sarah's circle early on. Pat is a no-nonsense woman, retired and well connected with community life locally. She talks about Sarah and her circle:

> *'Sarah can't speak to us and the only way she can tell us about her life is by us being with her. Being in the circle gives us a way to link in with her and get a real sense of who she is and the life she's had and what that means. I know she is not my kin, but it isn't any kind of chore to be in her life and have her in mine. It feels very natural and ordinary to pop in and see her – it feels good to visit and I realise it's a privilege having her in my life. When we thought hard and long about Sarah's life experiences we imagined that in a different life she would have been a lady, so we went with that and followed the feedback from her. We bought her a china tea-set and lovely clothes. On her sixtieth birthday the circle of friends bought her a ruby ring and she's never had it off her hand since – that kind of thing is so important, you know; people who don't have family don't get special presents.'*

Some circles are a success because of the preparation that's undertaken to welcome old friends and family members into the person's current world and life. Many families will have found it hard to maintain ordinary contact with their relatives when they've been in institutions. Some family members will need to build up trust before they can follow the more ordinary patterns of other families. For example, Betty is Alice's sister and for a while after Alice moved into her own home, Betty would ask the staff about when it would be OK to visit and when not. That formal approach was very characteristic of the institutional places where Alice had lived. Eventually Betty realised that she can come when she wants and just drop by as she would with any friend or family member. She would be welcomed by Alice and her staff team too when she did that. In the end the feeling of *ordinary life* is not created by what Alice does or what the team does or what the family does but by the very nature of the interactions between them.

For some it's a big step to realise relatives and friends can visit whenever they want and stay as long as the person and they both want, and that they can even bring cakes or presents. It's another shocking indictment of our social service system that ordinary relationships have been so badly disrupted or even prevented by bureaucracies and by the coldness of some social care practices. There are also residual effects on how we all think. Veronica, for example, is a daughter and an auntie. She has these roles because of the family she was born into and because of the age she has reached. In order to fulfil these roles the team and circle had to support her to take actions like inviting her parents out for a meal, sending presents and birthday cards, baking cakes and so on. All these actions help cement her roles as a daughter and as an auntie, and the facts that she lives with cerebral palsy and uses a wheelchair, and that she's suffered from chronic low self-esteem, are no longer focused on.

A circle is a circle when all circle members benefit
Obviously, relationships are always about more than one person. Gifts and contributions travel in all directions and the trick is to look for all the giving and possible giving in the relationships and bring attention to them. It seems to us that

limiting your thinking so that circle members are seen as only there to make a difference to the supported person is a much less interesting view. For a circle to work then everyone, not just some, must benefit.

Matthew's circle is a good example. His is very different in size and shape to Sarah's. It's smaller, and appears from the outside to be more casual, though in fact it's very carefully constructed. We don't need to tell all of Matthew's story here but if we did it would bring tears to your eyes. It's perhaps enough to say that he's been moved from institution to institution over the years and before getting his own place with Getta Life he had hardly anyone who would stick by him or really go out on a limb for him. He was essentially alone, very isolated and understandably very cautious of strangers. Some of his life experiences appear to have been frightening and have left him feeling vulnerable with those he doesn't trust. Building a circle from scratch required a different approach to building Sarah's circle.

For Matthew, one small step in the process was asking a worker's husband, Laurence, to become involved. Sean, the father of a friend of the same worker's son, was also asked if he might like to get involved. Both men decided to give it a go. To help develop a relationship, Laurence and Sean would visit Matthew and do odd jobs around the house. It was thought that this would help Matthew differentiate them from the staff and also give them some reason for being there so that Matthew could approach them if he wanted, but on his own terms. It was essential that Matthew didn't feel obliged to greet them and also that he didn't associate them with his staff or carers. Nowadays you might find all three men sat around the kitchen table tucking into a curry and a beer or two. Everyone has gained in this – Laurence and Sean are also now friends.

Another poignant example of the power of circles concerns Sarah. When Margaret, a circle member of Sarah's, died, Sarah went to the funeral and Margaret's family were enormously pleased she had come, giving them some comfort at a sad time and reassuring them of Margaret's importance in the lives of others. Now Jagan has joined Sarah's circle and accompanies her swimming, which he had never done before. Sarah gives Jagan lifts to do his shopping and they have been away on holiday together. A beautiful mutual friendship has evolved from Sarah's circle.

John, who is a member of Jonathan and Zara's circle, summed up the joys of membership:

> 'I have seen them both become healthier and more relaxed and no longer dull as if life had broken them. Now there is something brighter about them, an aura of dignity. Being in the circle and seeing what the team does has restored my faith in human nature – positivity will overcome the negativity.'

Beyond the edge – asking for help

> 'I like the circle of support idea, it widens us and includes other people who have an interest so we are less blinkered.'
> – A family member.

For some of us (me included), one of the most difficult things we do as human beings is ask others for help. But asking is a crucial part of helping form circles and teams. In order to be a successful 'asker' you need to know what to ask for, and this involves representing the person and talking about them to others. Yet something often stops us making that step, of approaching others either individually or in groups. Perhaps there is a fear of being turned down. For people who have been supported in services distant from community, or people with reputations for being challenging, the circle probably won't develop without purposeful asking. Inviting people to join a circle and accepting that some will refuse the invitation is part of the work when supporting someone to develop their life.

**Every circle and team organises differently –
let it happen when it's trying to happen!**

Sarah's circle has evolved to have its own identity. Marjorie talks about that:

> *'If the right respectful attitude is there then it's possible to discover who a person really is – it's been a joy to discover that. Sarah has blossomed and become a different woman – now she always looks nice, lovely clothes and nails. Where she was before she looked like a patient – why? It costs very little, yet the results are self-confidence and self-worth, so important.'*

Marjorie's take on Sarah's story reminds us that circles can be a supportive way of helping a person grow and flourish. In order for that to happen a certain type of relationship has to emerge. The right approach, it seems, is not to have preconceived ideas about what the circle should do or what the roles of circle members should be or how the circle should develop, but to notice what's happening naturally and look to see if you can support that to happen more.

> *'Being in the circle is not like a staff and service user relationship, it's like person-to-person....In some services if you don't quite fit into their box then you won't do very well. At Getta Life there isn't a box, and because there isn't a box there's a deeper way of thinking. In Sarah's circle we could find out what she meant through her sounds and emphases; we had to work hard to learn it all right, but then she began to trust us and other people around her – the changes have been wonderful and I feel proud to have seen the change.'*
>
> – A member of Sarah's circle.

Circles are a great way to help give relationships a place to grow in. *'It's strange to say this,'* says Marjorie from Sarah's circle, as if she is embarrassed to use such emotive language, *'It's strange to say this and use the word "free", but this is what Getta Life have done, they have freed people. Yet when they've done so they've also given a lot of support in that freedom.'*

> *'Claire's circle meetings are always a fun affair; we eat, we dance and we laugh a lot. We plan nights out together and they're always relaxed and comfortable; just a group of friends hanging out together. Recently when Claire had a difficulty and there was a serious risk that she might lose her home, her circle worked very effectively as a team to protect her interest, presenting a united professional and effective support.'*

– A member of Claire's circle.

CHAPTER 4

How Circles and Teams Reflect the Person

KEY MESSAGES

- ☑ Great support means not leaving relationships to chance.

- ☑ Circles are intentional ways of creating a mini community around the person – to help them learn about who they are and how to be in relationships with others.

- ☑ Teams and circles both require thought and care in how they are set up and how they evolve over time.

- ☑ We get to know ourselves through the people we are closest to.

- ☑ Everyone needs to have others who believe in them.

- ☑ Ask the right people in the right way and circles will happen.

- ☑ It's always a two-way street – everyone benefits.

- ☑ Sometimes it's not clear who is learning from whom and who is doing the supporting. That's fine.

- ☑ There are principles but not one method that works for all – consider each situation differently.

- ☑ Circles and teams thrive on sharing – whether that's food, dancing, music or conversation.

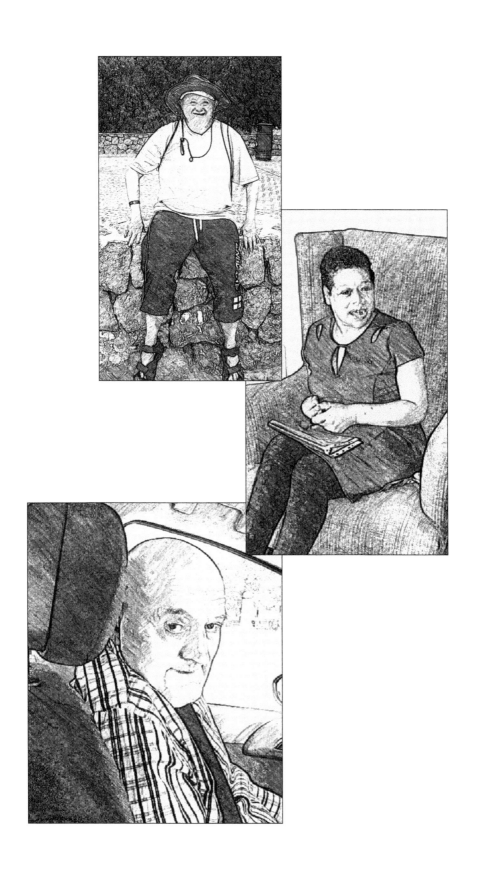

Chapter 5

Discovery

Written by Julie Smith of Getta Life

Most of us like surprises and through discovery there are many. The braver we are and the more we believe in the possibilities that life holds, then the more discoveries we can make. I like the idea that we can discover things as we go through life; new places, new insights, new pleasures, new talents and new people – that we can't predict what we are yet to discover!

For all these reasons discovery is part of the key to supporting people to grow and develop, as well as ensuring that they're supported to lead meaningful and fulfilling lives.

Curiosity

At Getta Life we work to develop a culture of curiosity, encouraging staff to look and think and be curious, because people are interesting. Staff need to recognise that the people they support have been different at various times in their lives, and that although they are as they are now, they also have a past and a future. We need to support people to discover themselves, and the essence of who they are.

So how do we develop a culture of curiosity?
The staff know that we will ask the question, 'Why?' a lot. They know that in their supervision and team meetings they'll be asked to think about things and to answer questions like *'How come?'* and *'What have you discovered about the person you support this week?'* Often team meetings involve reflective exercises asking the team to think together about the person they support and about themselves. This may be through questions such as *'What have you noticed about the relationships you have with the person you support, with their family and with your colleagues?'* Or it may be through storytelling about a special moment or having a set amount of time to talk about the way they feel at work.

We should listen to the things we are told about people by professionals and paid staff, as well as give equal value and lots of attention to the stories that the person's family share. By listening to professionals and to the staff we can learn who likes the person and who doesn't, who is a good advocate and who is merely doing a job. We learn about what is working and what actions or processes simply don't make sense. We get insight into how life has been for people in other services and sometimes how not to do things from now on. By listening to family stories we often learn who the person really is and what has shaped them, about the family's values, traditions and experiences, about everyone's feelings and emotions and how other services have affected the person and those around them.

Patrick is a guy always on the move. Movement seems an important strategy for him in managing his anxiety; it helps him feel more relaxed and settled. He likes to walk and move his hands. We know he is less anxious now because he doesn't pace so much in his home. Also team members have to be calm themselves; one team member felt badly treated by him and became on edge. As a result Patrick began to push that carer out because they were increasing his anxiety and they weren't the right person to be supporting Patrick. Now his team reflects his emerging nature of calmness. They also learnt by understanding his story that what he does makes sense. This all helps the team see Patrick as a person and not label him.

How do we listen to the right people?
Again I am considering the questions I often ask staff, *'Why are things done the way they are?'* to see if the reasons are purposeful and person-centred. I ask, *'What makes you sure that you're getting things right?'* and *'How do you check this out with the person?'* I ask *'Where has your information come from?'*

In the planning process when we first work with people there's a time to listen to their story in whichever way they and their families want it told. I see in the team's faces the discoveries that they experience while listening; the expressions of surprise, shock, empathy, insight, joy or concern. Planning also gives us the opportunity to imagine things that the person may wish to do. A lot of time is spent on dreaming, having properly listened to the person's story, and gaining insight into their gifts and talents.

We must also change the way those working with the person think about them and their family if we are to discover new things. This opens our minds to the reality that the views and interpretations of others are just that and not facts or givens.

We are able to change reputations if we believe both in the quest to discover the true person, and that they can be someone wonderful. Many of the people we support had been labelled as 'difficult', resulting in them suffering some terrible services, with their lives restricted in the name of risk management. They had been misrepresented and mistreated and in some instances abused. We had a lot of unpicking to do.

Their families, too, sometimes have reputations that are passed on by professionals. It's important that we don't trust these, but take the time to get to know each family just as we get to know their family member. Often these reputations are a consequence of people having been in conflict as they tried to achieve better services for their family member, or from a lack of trust and openness between the service and the family, leading to poor communication, assumptions and blame.

How do we challenge these reputations and ensure they don't continue to affect the person in the future?
First and foremost, we refuse to believe them! We advise our staff to think carefully about the words they choose to use when describing people and to challenge those who speak in a negative way.

We spend a lot of time learning about the person's history or their family's reputation and discovering how previous services might have given rise to those. We ensure staff understand that reputations can be unfair, underlining this by discussing what is wonderful about the person and their family. To help the staff understand the damage that labels can create, we use case studies that illustrate what used to be said about a person in contrast to how that person really is. When we begin to work with families we notice how past patterns could be perpetuated. We talk to families about the process; how we can help them get back to being a family, discussing levels of anxiety and trust. We ask what we can do to support them at the same time as supporting their family member. Everything is approached with a sense of curiosity around the differences between families and how each team responds to those differences.

When Minnie moved into her home she had a reputation for being uncooperative and loud, and complex in terms of her mental health. By contrast we found her quirky, independent and idiosyncratic. This is enjoyable and keeps us on our toes! On the day she moved, her brother Brian arrived with champagne to toast Minnie in her new home. He spoke to her repeatedly about it being all hers and how she could do what she wanted there, and that the staff were there to do things how she wanted them done. This inspired the team and they treat her like a princess.

On Minnie's first planning day, six members of her family came and the first hour was a social event while everyone caught up. The day was filled with noisy chatter, everyone shared family stories and Minnie was supported to develop an excellent plan. We discovered that one of her uncles had been an opera singer and that Minnie used to go and see him perform. We were aware that when Minnie is not so well she will sing in an operatic way; now this made sense. As a result we've bought tickets for her to go to the opera, with the hope this may turn into a regular event. Another family member helped us to think about Minnie being a woman and about being pampered; this led us to try a day at a spa and to buy glossy women's magazines. Since that planning day Minnie has enjoyed a birthday party with her friends from Getta Life and her family celebrating together; it was lovely to see Minnie's uncle dancing with Violet, one of the team. The level of respect and acceptance towards everyone was obvious.

Exploring

During Jonathan's planning day we were thinking about his gifts and the team members shared stories of how Jonathan has helped them. Boni said that when he was feeling lonely Jonathan patiently listened. Both Catherine and Martha shared about how in the evenings they chat with him and how easy it is to confide in him. I personally find him relaxing to talk to. We realised that Jonathan has the gift of being peaceful to be with. As a result of this we decided it would be excellent to support Jonathan in attending a relaxation and meditation class, where he may be of help and support to others. We tried contacting several classes but they didn't get back to us. Then we found a yoga class where the tutor wanted to find out more. He arranged to visit Jonathan at home to understand what we were asking. During his visit he listened very carefully as we explained what had happened during his planning day and said, 'It sounds like a lovely idea'. Jonathan went to his first yoga meeting the following Wednesday and it was comfortable for him even though it was his first visit. The atmosphere in the yoga meeting worked exceptionally well for him.

In Claire's team we did an art exercise where people were asked to draw something that represented change. We talked about our experiences and attitudes around change and what our pictures represented. We realised two things; firstly, that the struggles the team were experiencing were due to a lack of understanding of each other and their very different approaches to change. Secondly, that Claire was far braver than most of us and we needed to work in a way that reflected this.

We learnt from Alice's sister that when she was a child her family kept chickens and that Alice used to help her mum collect the eggs from their chicken shed. She joked that they'd had a lot of scrambled eggs, but that Alice had loved doing this. We decided to take Alice to see some chickens to gauge her reaction, especially as we were aware that she is scared of many animals. We discovered that she isn't scared of chickens! We also knew that Alice never used her garden, seeming to dislike it, and never went through the back door. So by reminiscing and observation we made a discovery, which resulted in us helping Alice buy some chickens and a coop. Now each morning she has a fresh egg for breakfast and on sunny evenings she enjoys sitting in her garden with a glass of wine watching her chickens.

Recently Catherine was supported to visit her family in France. They were in the process of getting a downstairs room ready for her but as it wasn't ready in time for her visit a gîte was booked nearby, which was advertised as accessible. When Catherine arrived, they discovered that the gîte wasn't suitable, so Catherine and her family went back to their home to see if she could manage. To everyone's surprise Catherine went up and down the stairs to bed every evening, achieving this through pure determination. But there was another discovery in store for us. This came through Gladys, one of Catherine's support team, when they were both staying in Catherine's brother's house. Gladys had the opportunity of experiencing Catherine's relationship with her family in a very different way. When they returned home, Gladys shared how Catherine was treated with great respect, enjoying hours of reminiscing and storytelling with her family. Catherine loves to share this with us, mostly through the use of family photos.

A while ago Karl needed to move home as the house he was living in was on a short-term let which wasn't going to be renewed. We supported Karl in the viewing of potential properties, the aim being for him to buy somewhere under a shared ownership scheme. Several of the houses Karl visited weren't right for him. We were very happy that he was able to show us the one he liked through appearing settled and by going into every room and staying in there for a length of time. Again, by including the person, and by being curious and observing, we discovered what was wanted and judged best by the person himself.

Don't worry

In order to discover new things we need to have a balanced view of risk by understanding and accepting responsible risk-taking as a way to support personal growth. We carry out risk assessments but only when there is demonstrable risk to the safety of the supported person or the team.

When I first met Rebecca the service supporting her at the time handed me a pile of risk assessments for every eventuality, from doing the shopping and travelling in her car to catching a train. I didn't want to ignore a situation that might be difficult for Rebecca, but nor did I want her to be controlled by risk assessments if they were unnecessary. It was a dilemma as I didn't know her well enough at that time. I met her mum and we talked through each one; she told me how they had come about and what she believed about the risk. We kept three of them and put the rest in the bin!

When I met Sally she wasn't going swimming and she would always have a shower, never a bath. I'd been told that she loved water so I wondered, how can this make sense? I asked the staff at the service supporting her at the time and they told me there was too high a risk. They felt that Sally might keep walking into the swimming pool and not stop before she was out of her depth and in the deep end, but as far as they knew she had never done this. They felt that she might lie down in the bath so that her head went underwater; again they were not aware that this had ever happened.

When listening to Sally's family memories Carol, her sister, told us a story of when Sally was a little girl. She often wandered off into the garden and her mum would be looking for her. Once her mum booked a photographer to take Sally's photograph and her mum dressed her up especially for the occasion. When the photographer arrived there was no sign of Sally. Eventually they found her sitting in a puddle splashing in the water and having a great time. This photograph was framed and given to her by her family for her new home. It's a really good reminder of the importance of water and play. Sally now goes swimming each week and enjoys a bath in her new home.

In working with someone to change their reputation, we must give consideration to who needs to know what: what information is given to other people and how this affects the way the supported person comes across. Thinking about how you introduce someone and the general information you disclose can make a real difference to how the person is viewed. Publicise success, talent and qualities and talk about how things can happen in ways that will work for the person, while going through difficulties and risks discreetly.

The impact of this approach to risk shows clear benefits that are refreshing for families who may have struggled with services that have limited their family member through fear. Felicity explains the way this has changed things for her and her sister.

> 'They started by revisiting the parts of her life she used to enjoy. The old staff team couldn't get round to making that happen, as for them it involved lots of risk and planning. In these services her life simply shrank, while Getta Life just did it. They keep adapting and changing; they review things daily and make tiny adjustments, always looking at it from Claire's perspective.'

In answer to the question *'Is there a secret to what they do?'* the answer might well be, *'Learn quickly, be flexible, and change things.'*

Recently we supported Veronica to attend a conference. After it was booked we discovered that the support staff couldn't be there. Our initial reaction was one of concern as Veronica had never done anything without us by her side. Louise, her support team manager who could be there, planned to play it by ear and see how it went, saying that if it wasn't suitable they would come away. On their return from the conference Louise was very excited. She talked about how well Veronica had done, telling me that she'd been paid to do nothing that day! Veronica had found some other people with difficulties to be with who gave her the confidence and support to be there with them. She was extremely proud of herself and we are now working together to see how we can increase Veronica's opportunities for this kind of independence in the future.

What if?

Elizabeth, a member of Zara's team, was expecting a baby. It was a happy time and the pregnancy turned out to be a gift for them both. As Elizabeth got bigger, one day she asked if Zara could help her by walking to the shops so she wouldn't need to push the wheelchair. This was the first day that Zara walked outside her house without sitting down every few steps in panic. Their relationship meant that Zara wanted to support Elizabeth, and that she felt confident enough while with her to walk. The team celebrated Zara's achievement and she was justly proud – which in turn increased her confidence. The momentum and excitement grew as we watched Zara walk in more and more places. The trust she had come to feel in those who support her and the longevity of those relationships had enabled Zara after a long time to literally find her feet. She recently took part in the Race for Life, walking part of it!

Daniel has always found visiting the doctor, dentist or hospital very hard; often he refused to go into the consulting room or would leave the GP's surgery before he could be seen. The hospital said he had to come with two staff when he needed sedation for dental care as he wouldn't allow them to sedate him when he was supported by only one person. However, when Angela, his partner, was very ill and required hospital treatment, an operation and a stay in hospital he overcame all of these fears to support her. We discovered that Daniel had the capacity to manage all these medical-related issues when his role was to support Angela. He attended all her outpatient appointments with her, waited while she had blood tests, visited her every day following her operation and did a great job of supporting her. During this time he didn't complain at all about being in the hospital environment and coped with a lot of waiting around. This made us think. We had a light-bulb moment: what if Angela went with Daniel for his doctor's appointments and hospital visits? The discovery was how much we had to learn about seeing the wisdom of others in supporting each other. Daniel happily went into the GP's surgery when Angela went with him and allowed the GP to check his blood pressure and make an examination. When he returned to the hospital for his dental treatment he allowed the staff to sedate him because Angela was there. Angela now helps Daniel with all of his medical appointments and this works very well; her simply being there helps him to keep calm and enables him to get better care and treatment.

As Rebecca settled in to her new home and relaxed with her new staff team we discovered her sense of humour: it had been lost to her anxiety for some considerable time. It is lovely now to find that there are many occasions when she makes us laugh. When Rebecca moved in to her new home with her new team she wore only black clothes; she was not too interested in her appearance and never wore make-up. After a few months Rebecca relaxed into her new life and gradually started to choose different clothes. Then one evening she went to a friend's house and saw her friend being supported by her staff to wear make-up and Rebecca was happy to try it too. From that point she has chosen to wear make-up and a wide variety of differently coloured outfits. Best of all is how pleased she is when people notice and tell her that she looks great. She has discovered her beauty and is proud of it.

Discovery comes in lots of ways

Through following the principle that everything people do tells us something, like how people react to personal care, how and what they drink and how often, and how people sleep, then there is something to be learnt in all the everyday things. Through discovery and curiosity we can work out when to worry and what to worry about. We become aware of patterns and look for changes; we take these seriously as we try to learn more and more about the people we support. We need to make connections between things and look for insights.

Knowing people for a long time, and having real and right relationships that have longevity, all add to the process of discovery. Knowing that the learning never stops and that we are side by side with the person on a journey that will take us both to unexpected places is a strong foundation for good support.

When we first saw Patrick it was through a window. He had his nose pressed up against it from the outside, watching us sit with Matthew while he ate. We asked the carers why, only to be told that it wasn't his turn to be in the kitchen having lunch and so he was outside waiting. He was shut out in the garden until it was his turn. Understanding what has happened to people before in their lives helps us to understand how they are now. There is a reason for difficulties that may present themselves now, and eventually perhaps there is a solution. Where there is hurt we work towards safety, trust and healing.

Discovery also comes through adventure
We have supported people in taking part in activity holidays where they have enjoyed abseiling, canoeing, rock climbing and much more. We learn about each of the people we support and are always surprised at how people engage. Neil is a young man who is often very ill. He is frail due to his

health issues and because of this it would be easy to wrap him up in cotton wool. We decided to take him to Bendrigg, a residential activity centre: we were amazed by his bravery and how much he clearly loved the adventure. This year is the fourth time he has visited; as he got to the top of the zip wire he knew what was about to happen and gave us a huge smile of anticipation. It is important to develop the bravery of staff and their confidence to step into the unknown – not necessarily on a zip wire but with the support they provide. We must allow staff to make mistakes and to learn alongside the person they are supporting; we must expect staff to push themselves out of their own comfort zones. We need to be keen to discover things about ourselves as staff and as people.

The training that we deliver is designed to be challenging and to stretch people. At times we know that staff may be uncomfortable, but it's through this that they will grow. Every two years the teams have an Away Day together. They have a budget to use and must select an activity that they'll find a challenge. Together they can learn about each other and themselves.

Discovery through a culture of 'Yes you can'
It may seem obvious, but sometimes the only way to know if an idea is a good idea is to try it out. We agree to a lot of ideas, and this means that the teams are encouraged to think and to voice their theories. It leads to a sense of pride, motivation and autonomy for staff in their work and encourages creativity. This all promotes a culture of 'yes you can', which means that we think about *how* to do things rather than why we shouldn't. Words like 'bravery' and 'courage' are regularly used and people are helped to step outside their comfort zone when that is right for the person they support.

We found somewhere it was possible for people to go sailing; the facility had instructors and hoists and was part of the Sailability service. A large yacht took small groups of people on the water while someone sailed the boat for them. Lots of the people we support really liked this experience, so it was disappointing when they couldn't accommodate us any longer. After looking around we found somewhere else offering Sailability, but in a different way. They used small two-people dinghies which the staff would need to sail. An instructor would be on the water in a boat alongside them and they would learn as they went along. Several members of staff were seriously scared, but we expected them to try. After the first sailing evening everyone had enjoyed themselves hugely and staff were excited about the next time they would go. Catherine couldn't get over the fact that she had steered the boat herself; she was so proud. Robert said, '*I thought it would be very scary but actually it was fine.*' This gave us the chance to talk about having faith in ourselves and knowing that things are possible. Part of the way we encourage discovery is to expect the staff to be brave, but also to take each opportunity to talk about how to grow and what we learn.

Discovery can happen at any age
Patrick is seventy years old and he is discovering lots of things just as we are discovering lots about him. What Patrick likes most is walking and travelling. Movement helps to ease his anxiety and so his team have spent lots of time walking and visiting different places. At seventy he has begun to discover England. One of the places he visited was the Old Trafford football stadium where there was a queue that Patrick went straight past; he had a look around the stadium and left. Getting the opportunity to be out and about a lot has helped to reduce his anxiety and enabled Patrick to move around his home in a way that isn't pacing; this in turn has led to him being more relaxed. The team has gained more insight into who Patrick is, with more time to learn about his preferences. An example: at times Patrick would watch the TV and his team thought maybe he would like to go to the cinema. Each week they go and try a film. Sometimes he won't go in at all and sometimes he will watch for an hour; very occasionally he will see the whole film. We are trying to discover if Patrick likes the cinema and how we can support him to get the most out of it. Discovery

is about not giving up on things, and about keeping an open mind about what is possible.

Discovery happens when it's not expected
We recently had a lovely surprise when supporting Rebecca to attend the Getta Life Oscars Night. It gave us the opportunity to dress up and, because Rebecca had been discovering how to be beautiful, she was very excited to be wearing a dress, and heels too. We had never seen Rebecca dance, yet she took her dad on to the dance floor before anyone else and when it came to the end of the night asked, *'Can I stay here all night?'*!!

Discovery also comes from revisiting things you have tried before and re-thinking them. Recently we had a new member of staff join Claire's team. At a planning day we had talked about how we could give Claire natural opportunities to meet men. The new team member suggested a male hairdresser, but we were aware that the last time we'd tried to support Claire at the hairdresser's she had come home with the dye still on her hair – and not for the first time. We believed it was worth trying nonetheless, and it has worked out very well. Claire now really likes going to the hairdresser, he makes her feel special and advises her on colour and style; she looks fantastic and her sister is even envious.

Getta Life agreed to take a social work student on placement and part of the student's remit was to do some group work. We decided to ask our student to set up and run a men's group. This was to be a short-term project because we had some reservations about setting up groups; we wondered how they would be person-centred and were concerned they may feel too much like a day service. We were surprised by how much people liked it! When the student placement finished the men wanted to continue with the group. Gari, a staff member, gave it some thought, decided he might be able to take the group forward, and presented his ideas in a proposal. The people we support decide if they want to go or not and they all take part in their own way. Interestingly, the men's group has played a large part in developing our sense of community.

Often staff see things that we can't because they spend their time with the people they support and hang out with them in many different places. Karl's team began to talk about how Karl was observing Zara, who is also supported by Getta Life, and they also felt she had noticed him. It wasn't something that we would have spotted ourselves or would have thought to look for. The teams wanted to support Karl and Zara to see each other more often on their own rather than in a group. It turned out to be a good idea.

Discovery through having your own home
For Sandra, discovery about having her own home has meant that she has shown us lots of things that she can do and communicate to us what was hidden before. Now she shows us when she wants to watch TV; she'll ask us to switch it on by sitting in front of it and making a noise. She shows us that she wishes to go out by going out of the door by using the key. These two changes also offer a bigger, more significant message – that Sandra now feels she has the autonomy that's associated with having your own home.

For Sally, finding out what it means to discover 'home' also means discovering new sounds for communicating that she'd like to watch TV. Talking to her mum on the phone, going out of her front door with her key; it's like she is taking the lead in her life for the first time. At the start, and for a long time after, she was very fearful about lots of things; fearful that people would hurt her, she would always perch with her back to the wall with arms set on the chair ready to make a quick getaway if necessary. We don't know the history of this behaviour but we can see the results.

Discovery comes from adversity
When Neil's grandad got ill and was no longer able to take Neil out for the day it was important for Neil to find ways that he, his grandma and grandad could still have good days together. Neil and his support team began to pick up his grandparents and spent days together going to garden centres,

parks and pubs, taking canal walks and going to the theatre. At first it was a bit uncomfortable and we realised that although we thought we had got to know them we hadn't really spent very long periods of time together, and so what we knew was limited. The days out now are a pleasure for all of us and the confidence and trust that Neil's family have in his support team has greatly increased. We noticed that when they are worried about things they talk to us less, and so now if they're quiet we find a way to ask if something is wrong. These days we know that we need to ask – and they are more comfortable in letting us know their concerns. This means that their day-to-day anxiety about Neil is kept at a reasonable level and greatly reduced from earlier times.

When Karl broke his ankle we were worried he would struggle as he had to stay in hospital for several days while the doctor decided whether he needed surgery. What actually happened was that Karl showed us that he knew exactly how to be a patient and settled into ward life and being looked after, with all of our anxieties proving unfounded.

Discovery comes with time
We can't expect to discover just by asking questions – for a start how do you know what questions to ask? No, to get to know people you have to spend time with them. People show us the obvious but for other, more important details people wait until they trust us and are relaxed. The longer we know people for, the more we discover. The time also has to be right; to make discoveries about ourselves we need to be ready. It is easy for us to see what others could do differently but we know they need to work it out for themselves. It's up to us to create opportunities and challenges that encourage self-discovery.

Every team manager has been on a listening skills course and each one got something different from it. Some managers have gone on to do further counselling training because of how much they learnt and what it brought out in them. Some have grown in confidence in a way they didn't expect; others have learnt techniques to help them in their communication with others. All learnt a bit more about each other, strengthening the manager's group and, most importantly, they all discovered something about themselves.

Discovery also comes from not giving up on things but accepting it may be some time before they work. For instance, there have been a few occasions when we've managed to get Veronica to go swimming. Once she was in the water she loved it, but she still doesn't like the thought of going or using the hoist. Her mum tells us that as a little girl Veronica loved the swimming pool they had in their back garden, but that while she lived in a residential home something happened that put her off and no one knows what it was. When Veronica has been swimming she is always excited to tell people that she's been and seems proud of herself, yet when we try and go again she quickly says, 'No'. The team keep trying and hope that one day Veronica will look forward to swimming regularly.

When Rebecca moved into her new home we were over-enthusiastic about all the things she could now do and we tried to move forward too quickly. We swiftly realised this and slowed down, letting Rebecca take the lead. A year later Rebecca has begun doing more and more of the things that we tried to begin with. It's her time now.

Recently we have been pleased to find that Philip is sitting at the table with us during the team meetings and is happy to share his mealtimes with his friends and team.

We know that this is now OK for him as he shows us clearly when he is content.

I used to worry when Catherine had long periods when she preferred to stay in. I wondered if we were doing something wrong, if she was unhappy. When I asked her she would say she was fine. I never felt sure. I noticed recently that this pattern coincided with wintertime and we talked about how her family had done things. I smiled and said, *'Guess you'll start to go out again when the weather is better,'* and she gave me a grin that said, *'At last you understand'*. We don't worry any more; instead we find lots of nice things to do at home.

When Tari first began her work with us she was

over-professionalised in her way of working. She had worked for the NHS and was just beginning her social work degree. She started at Getta Life in Minnie's team; we thought she might work well with her as Tari had experience of mental health services. At the time Minnie hadn't moved into her own home and was living in an NHS short-stay facility while waiting for the purchase of her home to go through. Tari was very uncomfortable there and really struggled to see Minnie as the wonderful person that she is. The context of the service she was in got in the way for Tari and she wasn't able to form a relationship in the way we wanted her to. As it was really important to Minnie to get the right team around her, we decided to move Tari. Tari has now been working with Alice for some time and has joined us on many training days. She has had regular supervision and worked alongside some of our superb staff. I remember clearly the moment when Tari told me she'd realised what we were setting out to do and she could see that we'd got it right for people. She talked about the questions it raised in relation to what she'd done before and how she can now see what was wrong.

When Phyllis began her work with us, for some time we had concerns as to whether she was working in a person-centred way. She was supporting Sally and there were things happening that Sally's family were uncomfortable with. It seemed that Phyllis was prioritising tasks rather than building a relationship with Sally. There were many instances when we talked about how we wanted her to do her work and I could see that each time she tried to adjust her way of working but never quite got it right. Phyllis came to Sally's planning day and listened to her family tell her story and share their experiences and dreams. We did lots of team exercises designed to help us think about our relationship with Sally and to discover her positive reputation. There were two people in the team who had been with us for a long time and who I knew would always work in a relational way, so I asked them to help Phyllis. We reflected on the gorgeous moments with Sally, about what we were learning, about how to play and why playing is more important than ironing. Phyllis has worked hard to understand how we want her to go about things and now has a lovely relationship with Sally. She is happy to talk about her learning and what Sally has taught her about support work.

Discovery in training

While we work to discover more about the people we support we find that we discover just as much about the staff and ourselves. Reflection is a key part to everything we do, as is giving and receiving feedback. Training is delivered in a way that encourages people to question who they are and the impact they have on those around them. It also encourages staff to look at the things they've learnt about themselves from the person they support. For some staff this journey has been amazing and they have found the inspiration that's allowed them to develop.

We offer training that we feel will encourage and support staff in thinking about the aspects of life that are hard to contemplate; for example bereavement and emotional literacy. They are invited to recognise and respond to the common humanity that underlies our emotions.

Training starts by all new members of staff going through induction. This process enables us to see what assistance each individual member of staff may need. It facilitates their understanding of our expectations around the way they offer support, and the values that underpin our approach. Often we see looks of discovery on new staff members' faces when they begin to understand what is expected of them and the role that building relationships has.

Sue and I attend staff training as course attendees, which gives us the opportunity to learn about each other and from each other. This approach demonstrates the importance of openness that is an overarching ethos of the company; that it really is 'about everyone'. It also models very clearly the need for us all to be in relationships and to be open and honest in our work. It ensures the managers are known and are approachable; it's also exposing and reveals us as individual human beings and so fosters trust. As a group of staff, the more we know and understand each other the better our team work will be. The closer the Getta Life community becomes, the more we are able to support each other, and the more open to challenge we become. We have noticed, and external trainers have commented, on how committed to learning the Getta Life staff group are. It is evident that members of staff are engaged and put effort into their involvement on training days. They are curious and enthusiastic, seeing training days as purposeful and motivating.

CHAPTER 5
Discovery

KEY MESSAGES

- ☑ Be brave; you have to try something to see how it will be.
- ☑ There's always more to discover; we can never know all there is to know.
- ☑ Everyone has the capacity for growth and development.
- ☑ Curiosity is an important quality to develop.
- ☑ Reputations and labels tell you more about the service than the person.
- ☑ Spending time with people is the only way to discover the relationship you can have with them.
- ☑ Believe in possibility.
- ☑ Ask 'How can we?' and encourage creativity.
- ☑ Developing an understanding of yourself is crucial.
- ☑ Follow the principle that everything people do tells you something.
- ☑ Explore people's gifts and dreams.
- ☑ Listen to the person's story.

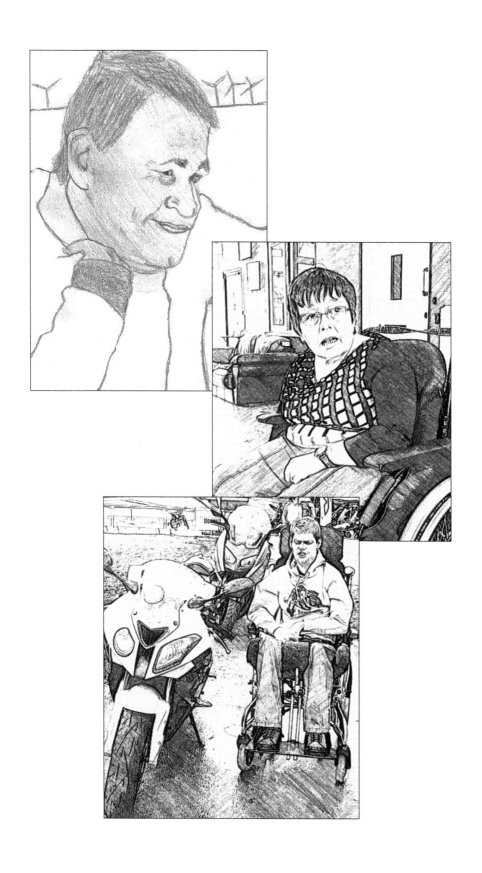

Chapter 6

Purpose and Intent

Written by Pat Black of Diversity Matters

Getta Life was founded because Sue and Julie had a vision that life could be very different from how it usually is for people who are labelled or thought of as having significant learning difficulties. They have never wavered from this purpose, and that's what Getta Life is able to offer to the people we support today. Yet we know that a positive, different life for people will not happen just because you want it to, or because you have an individualised service. What we know is that it requires unremitting attention to bring out the best in all the people involved.

Not only do Getta Life wish to bring out the best in people, they also believe that everyone is capable of more; every person can grow and develop and become a better self. This resolve is part of what keeps the organisation on track. Sue and Julie are committed in the way they work and support their staff to work. They make difficult decisions look easy because they are uncompromising in holding to their values and principles.

The information in this chapter is crucial not only to appreciate why Getta Life is successful but also to understand the detail of how to support people well in everyday activity and support them towards having substantial lives. Many people with learning difficulty labels have had much of their time wasted, waiting to be seen by specialists, to be assessed, to be fixed or made ready. People's lives are often put on hold while these things happen, giving the impression that their time and their lives are not important. Rarely are such people seen as having a deeper purpose in the world.

This chapter is an antidote to this way of thinking. Sue and Julie have consciously created a culture that says 'every person matters' and 'every aspect of that person's life matters'. This includes every detail of life from getting up in the morning to going to bed at night, but it also includes the big questions we all have about life, 'Who am I?', 'What is my purpose in the world?', 'How do I fulfil it?'. Cultures are formed by beliefs and Getta Life has a culture where everyone has a purpose, everyone is needed in the world, and that the role of support is to assist people to find that purpose and to experience being needed. This *does not* happen by accident. Instead, each and every step has to be turned in a specific direction and needs to have a reason behind it. There is a deep intent behind each action, and that is moving towards discovering a person's purpose in the world.

Person-centred planning

Person-centred planning has been both the philosophy and the way of working that has underpinned all of Getta Life's support to people. We fully believe in the planning process, and this has been at the heart of our operation. Every person that we support has a person-centred plan. People are supported in having a planning day each year until their lives are settled and on track, when we adjust the frequency to what is required. This will be different for each person supported. We're also considering holding a celebration day each year with each person.

Do regular, purposeful person-centred planning that is well facilitated by an external person

---

The planning day is always facilitated by someone outside Getta Life and is someone we trust to do it well and sensitively. When we first started out we had to consider very carefully who would have the right skills and values to support people and their families through this process. They needed to be able to facilitate in a way that not only helped staff to understand the person better, but also helped them to reflect on what they knew about the person and how this knowledge could be used to develop the person's life.

We were blessed in the early days with Carole and Guy who both more than met our brief and worked to facilitate the planning days in a sensitive and person-centred way. We've been able to use what they began as a template for successful planning days today.

The days are set up specifically to suit the person. For example, Sarah's planning day is always somewhere quite stylish and refined; for the last few years her day has been at Ryton Organic Gardens with a posh lunch for all of her circle of support and staff. Karl's is at his home with his family and then everyone goes to Frankie and Benny's for something to eat.

Rituals and routines have developed around the planning day. We help the person to think about whom they want to invite, and when they can't say we talk carefully to them and think about who are the right people to include. People send out formal invitations and everyone replies to confirm their attendance or not. Sometimes planning days are at the weekend if this makes it easier for families to be part of the process. The majority of those invited come, and are very excited to see and hear about the progress people are making. They also enjoy the twin opportunities of getting to know the staff better and of helping us work out how to better support people.

There is always a part of the planning day put aside to discuss and celebrate the person's gifts and talents, and each plan provides us with more new discoveries to add to the list. Each person has a giant poster displayed in their home, with their photo and their gifts and talents on it. These are very important as they are wonderful affirming messages; it also helps new support workers to quickly see the value in the person even as they first meet them. This is particularly important as some of the people we support have been labelled as being challenging or having complex needs. We believe it is paramount that who the person is gets seen very early on in the relationship with the support staff.

We also believe the people we support are enormously proud of their gifts and talents and enjoy having them celebrated. They show how proud they are when we read out the list or comment on some of their talents.

Stories about planning days

Finding home again: Sandra (in Sue's words)
At Sandra's sixth planning day we had been supporting her for seven years and it was incredibly moving for Sandra's mum, and for me, to be able to reflect on how much Sandra's life has changed and how far she has come. For example, Sandra now has her own car – but when I first met her ten years ago it took me all morning to persuade her to get into my car to go out, and she shouted for most of the journey. Now if her support staff say, *'Come on, Sandra, we're going out,'* she often races them to the car and wins.

Sandra now goes into her kitchen and helps herself to food and drink, and she loves to watch and help at mealtimes. When we first met, her fridge was tied shut.

Sandra now has a real sense of home and is beginning to be how she was when she lived with her mum, before she went away to live in an institution. How wonderful for Sandra's mum to see this and to see the Sandra she knew return. We should never underestimate the importance of home; it has taken Sandra more than two decades to find home again even though she left the institution twenty years ago. Life in the community isn't better unless you have a sense of home and safety.

Knowing people care about you: Matthew (in Sue's words)
Matthew almost died from pneumonia during the second year that we supported him. The planning day that followed this time was very solemn and sombre as Matthew was still recovering. We felt we needed to plan how to support him through his recovery and how to avoid any further traumatic hospital admissions. I remember Matthew going to sleep during the day as he was so weary, and me wondering whether we were doing the right thing by trying to plan at all. On reflection, it was the right thing to do as I think Matthew heard how committed we were to supporting him and how frightened we had all been that he might die. Matthew's planning day a year later was a complete contrast; he was robustly healthy and living a great life. He has chickens in his garden that he feeds twice a day and he sells their eggs. Matthew has released himself from the sofa and confidently goes out every day. Now, he has several close friends and is teetering on the edge of falling in love! Again, how brilliant to have shared the journey so far with Matthew and to appreciate how hard a struggle it has been for him. We should never think we can heal someone – we can set the right conditions for healing and we can be supportive, but people have to heal themselves. It is relationships that matter and these are what have most helped Matthew to heal himself.

In the story above about Matthew, Sue says that relationships helped Matthew to heal himself. Yet that only happened because of slow and purposeful actions intended to help people be available for a relationship with Matthew. This is easy to say but can be very difficult to do. Matthew has been very badly hurt in the care system. He was institutionalised as a teenager after one of his parents died, and lived first in a hospital, and then when it closed, in one of the worst group homes we have ever seen. He was neglected and abused. We will never know exactly what happened to him, but we do know he was emotionally wounded and experienced few, if any, nurturing relationships over a thirty-year period. So when Sue first met Matthew she was direct and honest with him and didn't conceal or lie to him about anything. This wasn't easy, but she knew that to build a sustainable long-term relationship he would need to be able to trust her. She didn't assume that he would or should trust her, but that she would need to earn that trust, and that he would, quite justifiably given his past, be very suspicious and very slow to trust. She assumed it would take a long time. This sounds obvious, but it isn't; many of us discount the wounds people have suffered. We know that it can be very painful to acknowledge someone's past, especially if they've been hurt by institutions or systems set up to protect. But if we're going to help people find their purpose we need to know what shaped them and who they really are.

Matthew's team was created with this in mind. One of the first staff members to be appointed was Philomena. When Matthew first lived in his own home he rarely went out and he spent hours sitting on the sofa with Philomena, playing with her hair. Sue and the team talked together about what they were learning and felt that this time with Philomena was productive, that they were forming a relationship and that Matthew was dictating the pace and nature of the connection. This was a very important step in building trust. Sue did a lot of work with the team to help them find ways to be at home with Matthew without being bored so they could actively wait till Matthew was ready to go out, however long that took. But they undertook this with an attitude of not giving up and not assuming it was for ever. They kept offering opportunities and gently supporting him to try, and if it failed, then not blaming or judging him but trying again with the same attitude. It took three years and no one gave up, no one thought it time wasted; it was time intentionally spent on relationships and on getting conditions right for Matthew to be able to heal.

Getta Life also employed a person-centred therapist to work with Matthew on his past. This is an unusual step for people with disabilities who don't use words, although it's a very common route for people who have suffered trauma but don't carry disability labels. The therapy allowed Matthew a place and a time to work on the past, and it showed him that people appreciated his pain and suffering. Again this was an intentional part of knowing that Matthew would need an opportunity to come to terms with the past in order to move positively into the future. It is not enough to assume he will get better or to get him on medication; too much of his life has been spent waiting for things to happen.

Gradually over time this purposeful attitude that's underpinned all the work with Matthew has led to the point where he has stable long-term relationships with people who are his friends; his staff team and other men.

Veronica
Veronica wanted to have her ears pierced but she knew that her mum wouldn't want her to; initially she was saying she couldn't because her mum wouldn't let her. We talked about what she could do. First, we looked at doing it anyway and upsetting Mum. Veronica didn't want to do this. Then we looked at not having them done. She didn't want to take this course either, so we asked Veronica who could help her talk to Mum, and she chose her sister. We supported Veronica in asking her sister to help her discuss the issue with her mum, and between them they got Mum's approval. Veronica had her ears pierced and now wears beautiful gold earrings.

Chris
Chris was looking for a service to support her daughter, and was interested in Getta Life. Chris works in a college that offers courses for people who need support and so comes into contact with a lot of people with learning difficulties and their

support workers. She noticed that the people supported by Getta Life were always well dressed and smartly turned out, and that they ate good food and always had a reason for what they decided. If people were late it would always be for a good reason; for example the person was having fun in the bath this morning, so it took a little longer. If they went for coffee in the college canteen it would be a social time, with a sense of togetherness. Chris also noticed that people supported by Getta Life were always doing something else later in the day, not just going to college; and that people were not all doing the same things. She rightly saw this as evidence that people were experiencing opportunities to grow and develop in lots of different ways.

Karl
Karl gets very excited by all kinds of transport and shows this by making loud and excited noises. At a bus stop Karl and his support worker Nikki were waiting for an approaching bus with a lot of other people and everyone was looking nervously at Karl. Nikki said loudly to Karl, *'Isn't it great to be so excited by the bus, Karl?'* and everyone at the bus stop relaxed. This intervention shows that Nikki was noticing the atmosphere and had the intention of relaxing people without putting Karl down or suggesting he should stop the noise. This is an aspect of knowing what you are doing and having a reason for it. It's very different from saying, *'Be quiet'* which isn't helpful to either Karl or the other people at the bus stop.

A truly purposeful organisation

Of course, this doesn't only apply to the people supported. For the organisation to be truly purposeful it has to apply this thinking and approach to all the staff. A mistake that is often made is to assume that the only important people in an organisation are the people using the service. This doesn't work because if staff aren't treated well then they'll be unhappy and not able to support the person properly, and might even leave. Again this seems obvious but is rarely considered elsewhere in the detailed way that Getta Life demonstrates.

This attitude of thinking and reflecting about everything permeates the whole organisation and is supported in many different ways, some of which are listed below.

Being person-centred – really person-centred
One of the important things about Getta Life is its commitment to person-centredness in a way that can sometimes be sidestepped by organisations. To Getta Life staff, being person-centred doesn't simply mean following the person's lead. Most of the people supported have limited life experiences so they can't make suggestions or put forward ideas about ways in which they could improve their lives. So Getta Life encourages staff to always imagine a substantial life for the person where they have friends, interests and activities.

When we first began supporting Alice she found going to the theatre quite difficult as she hadn't had that experience and didn't know what she was expected to do. For a long time she would see a bit of the show but then be asked to leave as she started making loud noises that disturbed others.

But we could see that Alice was enjoying the performances, so we looked for ways to help her stay quieter, for example ensuring she had toys to hold and ice cream to eat, and we kept on taking her and leaving when we needed to.

Now when Alice goes to the theatre she sits and laughs quietly, she claps when others clap and she enjoys watching the whole performance; in fact the theatre is one of her biggest pleasures.

Team meetings
In most team meetings we offer a personal development exercise for the team and tailor this according to what issues the team is currently dealing with. It may be doing something fun together or to help us get to know each other better, or to understand something more clearly or gain a deeper

insight into something that the team is struggling with. These exercises invariably help everyone to understand each other better and lead to enhanced support. Examples of these might include asking people to think about their experience of leaving home. How do they know someone is happy? How are they doing in relation to each other?

Sometimes exercises are designed specifically for a team where Julie or Sue want to challenge or change something. For example, in Daniel and Angela's team they looked at the importance of play and of being able to make a mess to ensure the team didn't try to be too tidy! In Sarah's team they looked at how they would like their life to be when they are sixty, and who do they know who's over sixty and what their life is like. Sue specifically spoke about her mum who is very active and very busy looking after horses and riding them competitively. This ensured that Sarah's team didn't see her as too old for some things and limit her choices and opportunities.

This approach was used at one of Karl's team meetings when there was a need to clarify whether he was happy and well supported as a neighbour had made an anonymous complaint. Karl doesn't use words to communicate and has a unique, exuberant style of communication. Anyone spending any time with him can't fail to be excited alongside him.

Sue began the team meeting by asking the team how they know Karl is happy. While his team spoke Karl stood in the middle of the room and, as he listened carefully to what everyone was describing, he laughed and tapped his foot on the floor. For Karl this was a skilful way of saying, 'I'm fine'. This approach enabled Sue to ascertain what was going on and put the concerns raised into perspective. It also meant she could confidently inform social services that all was well.

In some team meetings Julie reads out an excerpt from the book *Power Tools* by David Hingsburger. *Power Tools* gets you thinking about who we are and the power we have, suggesting that power is the most important issue that care providers need to consider on a daily basis. Recognising that without intent we can end up doing things that affect the dignity and self-esteem of the people we support, we bring awareness to our power and consequently reduce the possibility that we will abuse it.

After reading the extract Julie asks the staff to share their thoughts around power and relationships, leading to insightful discussions, continued awareness and learning how to work in a way where staff don't take control. Julie is eclectic in her influences; she also used the same process with a piece of music from the Mary Poppins stage show called *Anything can happen if you let it*. The lyrics convey some powerful messages about growth and opportunity. These approaches are used with much thought both to what the person being supported needs and what the team needs to consider.

Team away days

The team away days are another example of how things happen with intent. The nature of the team means that people work one-to-one and therefore don't spend long periods of time together – except for a team away day. Each team has an agreed amount of money to spend and can choose an activity to do for the day; if they want to they can include the person they support. The activity has to present a challenge and therefore give staff the opportunity to learn about themselves and their colleagues, while offering a fun day out and a time to relax as a group.

Some examples of things staff have done in their teams are: sailing, go-karting, dance lessons, tree-top assault courses and indoor parachute jumps. We learn a lot about people in this way.

Meaningful supervision for everyone

Supervisions, appraisals and personal development are all part of the purposeful work to support staff and help people to grow and develop. The way we practise supervision has developed over time. We began with an agenda: 'What's going well?', 'What are our training needs?' – and so on. Over time, as we gained experience and insight, it became more reflective and questions became more challenging. Recently we've introduced a system of observation, reflection and mentoring.

Currently staff undergo a reflective supervision one month, a standard supervision the next month and a piece of observed practice with critical reflection in the third. The way we deliver supervision, mentoring and coaching support is changing and evolving as the work grows and becomes more complex.

The reflective supervisions have opened a window for us into how the staff perceive their work and the person they support. They have been extremely valuable in enabling us to check how people are doing their work and helping them to think deeply about it. We ask twenty questions. Here's a sample:

- What has the person you support taught you about life and relationships?
- How do you contribute to togetherness in Getta Life?
- How have you helped a colleague or the person you support when they've been struggling?
- What are you doing at work when you have the most fun? How do you make sure fun is part of your work?
- Describe a time when the person you support was angry. How did you support them to express this anger and get through the day?

Our twenty questions are changed each year so there is variety and choice. Before supervision the member of staff and manager each choose a question which is most relevant at that time and write at least two A4 sheets in preparation for their meeting. Before setting the question the manager reflects on the current state of affairs with the member of staff, for example if they feel they're struggling with a certain part of their role they may direct them to the relevant question, or if there's a tendency for them to talk about themselves the manager may set a question which steers their awareness back to the person they are supporting. The time in supervision is spent sharing what each staff member has written and exploring what it teaches them. The following are quotes from some reflective supervision:

- I have learnt about life and relationships from two people I have worked with for years. My life has been about loss from a young age. When I was a boy some people I loved had all gone, I had to become a man at the age of twelve. I worked hard to look after my family. When I came to the UK I worked with Philip – I got a good welcome from him. From Philip I learnt that no matter what you look like or how you do things you can live a good life. Then I met Justin. He is full of love and he loves to be busy. I have learnt about moving and being happy with what I have.

- Terry has given me a lot of reasons to love my work. He has made me tolerant in situations – he has taught me to be patient and take life easy. Terry brings out a smile on my face whenever I need one. He has taught me what the meaning of love is all about.

- I admire Angela. She learns by looking and is very good at picking up feelings. She will take time to trust you and she tells you this when she meets you. She also tells you when you get things wrong. Angela is very protective of Daniel, she loves him very much and shows this by kissing him.

- I learnt that you live well with someone if you live with them the way they are and don't try to change or judge them, and that it is OK to forgive in a relationship.

As an organisation we are aware that sometimes when people become managers there can be a tendency to think you are there, you've made it and then sit back, taking your focus off your own practice. Everything is always changing, so the ongoing yearly reflection on the questions of how, when and where is paramount to ensure continued development and learning. Sue and Julie as directors acknowledge that in their own organisation they have a true freedom to be different, and to change things, and recognise their power to do so. The sister of Alice, one of the people Getta Life support, said, *'They have outrageous ideas that actually take off'*.

Staff appraisals – ensuring everyone is heard

Staff appraisals are conducted annually. They're carried out by Sue and Julie and ensure that every member of staff at Getta Life gets at least some dedicated one-to-one time with a company director. This practice was started after a team manager suggested it as a good way for staff to have a say.

Appraisals are a guided process of looking back over the last year's work and allow staff to look at progress, achievements and learning, both for themselves and the person they support. Appraisals show us how much a member of staff has improved their practice. They also help people to look forward and think about what next. Here are some examples of excerpts from appraisals:

- I have become a better listener
- I have grown in my approach and as a person
- If you invest in a relationship you get back what you give
- Being able to put the person's needs before my own
- I want to learn to be more person-centred
- I have learnt to be part of a team and to trust my ability and place within the team
- Working for Getta Life has enabled me to see what I'm worth
- I have learnt that people with learning difficulties are wonderful teachers
- I want to be more comfortable with my own way of working and not constantly looking for reassurance
- I have become more confident in challenging routine even for my kids and family
- I take pride in the way I look and present myself

- Since working for Getta Life I have appreciated how important it is for people with learning difficulties to be listened to and to express themselves

- I have learnt to listen more. I have learnt that it's OK to admit you don't know it all and to ask for help when you need it – it's not about one-upmanship

- I have developed a lot since working with Getta Life by making commitments, achieving goals and taking actions.

The way that appraisals are offered also reflects and honours the length of time members of staff have worked with Getta Life. For example, an individual's three-year appraisal is carried out over a meal at a venue chosen by the member of staff.

In recognition of a number of staff having been with Getta Life for seven years, we recently held an event at a superior hotel where everyone spent the day in comfort reflecting on their own journey. We used philosopher and mythologist Joseph Campbell's inspirational teachings; in particular, *'No one in the world was ever you before, with your particular gifts and abilities and possibilities'*. The day was facilitated by Diversity Matters.

The importance of continued training

Training focuses on relationships, togetherness, deepening insight, sticking with it and community connecting.

There is an element of personal development in all our training. Recently we added a three-day personal development course to our training plan, to follow our six-week listening skills course. Both these courses have had a profound impact on staff's knowledge, and their ability to work in a team and be empathic. This has improved the quality of support each person offers and helps staff to work in a more nurturing way. We have helped staff learn to drive, swim, reverse park, flower arrange, sail a dinghy – all as a way of offering more opportunities to the people we support. This flexible approach to personal development ensures everyone knows they matter and that they and their progress are important.

We work hard to determine what people need to learn after their basic induction training. At the beginning of each year we set out the training schedule for the next twelve months by reflecting on where we are now, the challenges over the last year, any recurring patterns or possible slips in provision and anything else that needs addressing that we're not comfortable with. We ask if our awareness is still aligned with the culture of support we set out to offer. Then we think about what needs to be put in place to be in line with these reflections.

Staff are encouraged to stop and work out what they have learnt from the supported person; not just what they've learnt about them but what the supported person taught the staff member. We encourage staff to observe every detail, take in what they notice and share it with others. To spend lots of time discovering who the supported person really is and what their gifts and talents are. To be persistent if something hasn't worked work out, think about why not, and never give up.

Examples of this approach in practice and its effectiveness can be clearly seen through observations made at the Getta Life Oscars Night. All evening there were small examples of high quality support and impressive teamwork.

- One man who had not known his team very long was dressed, like all of the men at his table, in a formal suit and was looking a bit hot and uncomfortable; he looked round, clearly unsure what to do. His team leader noticed and instead of saying anything simply took off his own jacket and hung it on the back of his chair. Another of the team did the same in a relaxed way, and after a few seconds the man removed his jacket and immediately looked relieved. This was excellent observation and non-intrusive support in action.

- Later at another table a support worker was sitting on his own with the person he supported as the others at the table had gone to dance. A small group of men including staff from a nearby table got up, came over and shook hands with them both; they all stood and talked together about the music and did a little bit of dancing by the table. Shortly afterwards the person went to the floor to dance.

- During the evening there was no one left alone with only their own team members. People moved around, greeted friends and danced with lots of people. One woman spontaneously went to dance and, recognising how unusual this was, a worker from another team danced with her while appreciating her dancing.

- The room was hot and often at such events you would expect to see a small group of staff outside smoking or getting away from 'work', but at this event there was only occasionally a worker and the person they supported together getting a little fresh air or having a short walk, before going back inside.

Interview and induction

Having the correct people working in the organisation and ensuring they know the right things about the person they support is vitally important to keeping the person-centred culture in place. When inevitably staff have to change, this is at the forefront of our minds.

The selection process allows us to look for people who align with Getta Life's values and principles and the interview provides the opportunity to sense how warm and open the candidate is. We ensure that the people they are applying to work with are involved in the interviews; family members too. However, over time families have come to trust us to make sure the very best people are employed and so they attend interviews less frequently.

We also have to be aware of the skills required in interviewing and selecting the best people; sometimes there can be a tendency to either choose someone like yourself or like someone you're used to, neither of which is always the most appropriate.

We place little emphasis on experience or qualifications and instead look for people we believe we can coach well. The team manager will tell the supported person's story fully and often to new staff to ensure they don't lose sight of who the person is and what their life has been like.

New staff spend time working alongside team members who know the supported person, with attention paid to the detail of everyday things, places and the people in the person's life. It is essential that all new Getta Life staff, even those who have a lot of training and experience, complete our own induction training.

We deliver the majority of this training ourselves, giving us a superb opportunity to get to know our new staff. It ensures that they're encouraged to think about all elements of the Getta Life approach to support. It gives us an opportunity to tell people's stories again and so keep their stories alive. During this period of time new staff are encouraged to build a relationship with the person they support. We ask them to think carefully about how they are doing this and to plan consciously to achieve a good relationship over time.

We talk a lot about this purpose and intent and we have many opportunities built into staff support so that this is always at the heart of what we expect from our staff.

Celebrating who the person is and working out the essence of that person

Getta Life promotes a special culture; a culture of working all the time to understand the uniqueness of each person, and to enjoy and celebrate it.

On one occasion Getta Life offered some training called 'The Right Relationship', facilitated by Diversity Matters. The teams and the person being supported worked together to think deeply about the person. Everyone was asked to think about good times they had shared and to carefully consider what had made that time special. Everyone did this several times with a number of different stories and tried to get to the essence of who the person is. Staff were then asked to imagine they had a guardian angel in their life and to visualise what the guardian angel would say was the supported person's purpose. This took a lot of reflection and led to some fascinating conclusions. Here are some of the purpose statements:

- Karl's purpose is to teach us that life should be lived to the full at all times. He shows us this by doing everything with enthusiasm, exuberance and obvious enjoyment.

- Catherine's purpose is to inspire us to believe anything is possible when you believe in yourself.

- Matthew's purpose is to teach us how to be brave and courageous. Matthew shows us that in order to be brave you have to have some fear.

- Angela's purpose is to teach people about relationships and friendships. Angela does this by vivaciousness and her infectious enthusiasm for life and people and through her partnership with Daniel.

CHAPTER 6
Purpose and Intent

KEY MESSAGES

- ☑ Recognise that everyone has a purpose and role in the world.
- ☑ Offer regular, focused person-centred planning.
- ☑ Keep awareness around power and relationships firmly on the agenda.
- ☑ If we are going to help people find their purpose we need to know who they really are.
- ☑ Give people the opportunities to grow and develop that are right for them.
- ☑ Apply the same values and principles to the staff.
- ☑ Offer regular supervision using a combination of guided questions, reflection and observation of practice.

Chapter 7

Community

Written by Andy Smith of Diversity Matters

Community is important to everyone; that quality of affiliation and acceptance we experience when we know we are in a shared world with other people, when we are recognised and appreciated and when we feel at home and belong. In this chapter we'll share some of the attitudes and ways by which Getta Life has tried to approach this question.

For a significant number of the people supported by Getta Life, a sense of community is provided by the organisation itself. Because addressing people's sense of isolation is urgent, it is essential that the organisation takes immediate action, especially if people have previously been excluded or alienated from their local community through prejudice, discrimination or because of the interventions of services. After all, it's a fundamental human requirement that we all need to belong somewhere and that we must be recognised and wanted. What this actually means in daily life can be different for each of us. For some people, being recognised by the couple who run the corner shop is a small but core part of the day. For others, it's that we belong in our home, or alongside our family, or in our street or our local area. For yet others, it could be that we find a sense of belonging through a workplace, or while volunteering, or through joining the darts team in the pub or being a member of a neighbourhood watch scheme.

Quite often these basic human feelings and experiences have been missing from the lives of the people we support. Some people have been painfully separated from their natural community, having been sent to live in specialist provision such as residential homes or long-stay hospitals. Helping people on the return journey requires a considered and dedicated focus; the person and the community alike may have doubts and concerns and reassurance might be necessary.

Where to start?

Here are three questions that help begin the journey into community: what are people's gifts?; what brings out the best in the supported person?; and how do you help the person get more of that? These questions help orientate the person, their family and the support team.

Sometimes when we first start to support people they have little idea of how to join in with others or what it means to belong. Through no fault of their own they have missed out on some relevant life experiences; they have no pattern for how to be in community with others. Perhaps no one has ever shown them, encouraged them or provided guidance. If that is to change then we need to work creatively and deliberately to help people learn how to belong and how to be part of their communities. This applies within the organisation and also in the communities and localities where the person lives. We have to provide the pattern, the encouragement, the links and connections. Sometimes we have to guide or sometimes we need to simply tag along and be there when people are finding their own way so they're not completely alone on their journey into community.

We also have to see the true person we are accompanying on this journey into the community. To see clearly we need to have the right attitude and the right relationship. This means believing one hundred per cent that everyone – that means everyone – has potential gifts, contributions and talents that are needed in the world in some way. Whoever accompanies or guides the person must believe in them, otherwise whatever you try won't work. So this focus on what we call 'gifts' is the critical Step One.

We know from experience that everyone has these qualities. A gift in this sense is principally a quality or essence in a person that draws others into relationship or community with them. It may be an intrinsic part of the make-up of the person; for example, Jonathan has the gift of being still and calm and centred. Karl has gifts of exuberance and joyfulness. Sarah has elegance about her. Each gift needs to be highlighted and emphasised so that others can see its value and how it might help in the quest for community.

Another key attitude or stance is to focus on what brings out the best in the person. This is a far-reaching, open-ended question. By following our natural interest in and curiosity about others, and discovering alongside them what brings out the best in them and us, we find that what we know this year will be only a small beginning compared to what we will have learnt by next year. It's crucial to ask, what brings out the best in the person, and how can we get more of that? It also holds within it an emphasis on the long-term possibilities of who the person might become and how they might live in the future. Other people are then attracted in and can embark on a learning process to see where that takes the person, and what new and exciting outcomes emerge from that undertaking.

> **It's important to spend as much time and thought in supporting people through friendships and relationships as on the rest of the job, even if there's little to go on at the start**

Working on the community is at the heart of our work
Step Two on the journey from the staff or supporter's point of view is a realisation that working on the community is not an add-on, but the crux of the work. Sarah spent most of her life in institutions and so when we first met her we listened thoughtfully and watched carefully to find out what brought her joy and engaged her interest. We noticed that she listened intently whenever she heard children's voices or if she heard children playing. The first time we saw Sarah smile was when she met Robert; he was four years old and Sarah was well into her fifties. So although all we had to go on was smiles and some time with one small child, we started from there. It's actually plenty to go on if you're concentrating on learning about the person as much as on achieving some other outcome. We thought about the connections we already had and this helped us make contact with the nursery that Robert attended. We explained that Sarah had time on her hands, was great with children and how could we make it happen for her to spend time at the nursery? We settled on a few ideas to get us and the nursery started; wheelchair painting – painting the wheelchair's wheels and then rolling the chair over large pieces of paper to make patterns – and helping to give out milk. And so Sarah started to visit Robert's nursery over the next two years and spend time with the children.

As Robert grew up this connection became weaker. For some time we were absorbed in Sarah's accommodation needs as she was in temporary housing while we waited for her house to become available. Sarah moved house three times in the next five years. When everything settled down the motivation was there to find new connections with children.

Then in one of her person-centred planning days, people talked about Sarah enjoying men's voices. By this time Robert was twelve so we asked him if he would read regularly to Sarah; this has continued most weeks and now Sarah goes to Robert's house and he reads to her there. Robert is now nearly sixteen and has a deeper voice; when Robert reads to her, Sarah leans in close to him and puts her hand out to be touched. She often makes a happy noise of agreement while she is listening and laughs a lot. She hugely enjoys this time, as does Robert.

Sarah found a different nursery to visit through Ollie, Robert's younger brother. She regularly goes to the library with her support worker and they take a story to the nursery each week. Her support worker reads to the children and then Sarah stays a while and watches the children play. Sarah has taught all the children at the nursery a lot about what having a disability means and she has a real sense of belonging there. The children and staff are always pleased to see her and are very welcoming; they give her birthday cards and share celebrations with her. Sarah in turn shows them her holiday photos and is supported to tell the children about her life. This is the core of good community-building; a situation where everyone benefits, learns and grows. Everyone appreciates being part of a diverse community and Sarah feels that she belongs and gets to spend time with children; the experience that brings out the best in her.

Supporting staff to make connections with the person and the community might mean stepping out of your comfort zone

---

Some staff teams struggle with developing community connections with the people they support. Charlie's team was one of them; we wanted to help Charlie to become aware of his community and to enable him to become a part of it. So some community-building training was offered.

We talked about what the training meant, explaining the value of helping Charlie to develop some new friendships in the local area. The staff found it difficult to see beyond the people he already knew, either since childhood or within Getta Life and his family. They understood it would be a great thing to do but were less clear about how to start. So as part of this ongoing training Julie agreed to support Peter, one of Charlie's staff team. They began by drawing up a community map, which included walking around the local area, going into the library, churches, community centres and shops, and talking to people and asking what there was to do locally. To start with, Peter didn't get it.

After gathering lots of information they discovered that a community café was starting up at the local community centre and they were looking for volunteers and customers. They took this information back to the staff team to talk it through, reflecting on Charlie's skills and what he could offer and what he enjoyed. This resulted in Charlie taking his DJ equipment to the community café Tuesday lunchtimes and offering DJ sessions. To begin with it was very much hit and miss as the café was quiet, and initially some of Charlie's support team felt it wasn't worthwhile, and maybe it was boring Charlie. But they persisted, knowing that it would need time to take off. Now Charlie has become a popular DJ; he knows lots of new people and has made a couple of friends whom he sees at the café. In fact the café coordinator asked him to DJ on other days – but he is too busy.

> **People need to learn that timing, trust and safety can be important foundations. We might need to set the right conditions and offer the right encouragement and keep trying even when it takes years**

When we first began to support Matthew he was distrustful of almost everyone he met and was reluctant to engage in life at all. Most of the time he preferred to stay on his sofa where it was safe or on a good day he might venture out for a trip in his car. The notion of community was far away and much too scary; Matthew had learnt that people hurt him so it was best to stay safe with just a few people in his life and try to work out how to trust them enough to be able to survive. It is hard to learn about community and the value of it when you aren't in it. Much of our initial work supporting Matthew was based on helping him to know how to trust us and when it's OK to trust people; this had to be done before he could get braver and venture out into the world.

We decided to help Matthew by inviting two men we knew from our own networks, Laurence and Sean, to get to know Matthew a little more to see what kind of friendship, if any, might emerge. We chose the people to ask with care and knew them to be very calm and quiet, not needy, and able to handle unexpected things that might happen during their visits. Essentially we wanted Matthew to learn that hanging out with others was a way to be in the world and that most people are safe. So this was our starting point for him.

> **It is important to provide options, ensuring they're not compulsory, and to help people follow their own inclinations**

There is a men's group in Getta Life; the men we support meet up once a week on a Thursday afternoon and do something together. Sometimes they take in some art, share music, or they go out. For example they visit Old Trafford, the Millennium Stadium, the seaside and anywhere else they fancy.

For a while someone would visit Matthew each week and tell him about the men's group and each week invite him to join it. Occasionally Matthew would get there but stay in the car. People would come out and say hello to him and let him know how pleased they were to see him. As Matthew spends a lot of time looking out of his window and his house was on the way to the men's group, people would often drive past his house and wait outside to see if he would join them. This was a strong neighbourly act and a good way for the other men to support Matthew. It also gave Matthew lots of messages that he was welcome in Getta Life and that people truly wanted him to join them. Over time Matthew got braver and attended the group most weeks, leaving the safety of his car and joining in. Each time Matthew managed to get out of his car and join the group he was given a spontaneous round of applause because everyone recognised how much emotional effort and energy it required.

Before long, people began to notice that whenever Matthew went to the men's group he sat by Daniel, another person whom we support. Encouraging workers to notice what's happening and who is bumping up against whom is a real talent; a skillset that is strongly supported, encouraged and nurtured in the staff teams. So quite naturally people thought that Matthew might like Daniel and so they arranged for Matthew and Daniel to spend a little more time together. The team always paid attention to see if these meetings brought out the best in both men and checked that they were giving positive feedback. Daniel would visit Matthew and they would share a curry together.

Daniel also tried to support Matthew to get to the book club run by Jonathan, another man supported by Getta Life. They would meet up and listen to the story together in between the book club meetings. Matthew didn't manage to get to the book club often and sometimes when he did he struggled to handle the intimacy of the reading group. Eventually because of how uncomfortable he found the club we helped Matthew to leave it and now he enjoys stories with his support team, and sometimes he and Daniel listen to stories together. It was clear that the intimacy of the book club together with a larger group was too difficult for Matthew to manage but he can manage to enjoy his books with Daniel.

> **Looking for community builders –
> and it might be the person you work for**

Daniel is a great community builder within Getta Life. He has also developed a good friendship with Philip; again this was noticed by support staff when Daniel and Philip met up at the men's group. Philip seemed to be very calm when Daniel was around and seemed very comfortable with him. This was tested out by supporting Daniel and Philip to spend time together; they both enjoy time rolling around on the floor together, giggling and making lots of noise. Philip has his own very special sofa which he guards jealously, and he only allows special people to sit there with him, Daniel being one of those people. Daniel has helped both Philip and Matthew to feel like they are part of Getta Life and that they are welcome. He has helped them both to feel valued, and to learn about relationships and friendships. Daniel's gift is wisdom about relationships and an inner calmness which means people find him really easy to be around. He is a fantastic relationships teacher to everyone.

> **Putting two and two together, going along with
> the ordinary things people do and seeing it as a
> learning process – you don't know where it will
> lead or what you will learn**

Alice loves magazines and she loves giving things to people. She has a generous way about her, and the inner qualities she has are certainly good generators of community feeling in those who meet her. When first supported by Getta Life she lived in a new development, a cul-de-sac with many older people of a similar age. We noticed that neighbours would ask staff about Alice and so people started putting these observations together. At the beginning, people only knew about Alice's pleasure in giving and her liking of magazines. They also knew about the need for neighbourliness in the street. It seems important to highlight this sense of mutual benefit in the thinking that is required for good community-connecting. It's not only that Alice has needs and gifts but the community has needs and gifts too. Alice's liking for magazines is a resource for the community, and the community needs more neighbourliness. It became possible to see the potential in helping her set up a magazine exchange in the streets where she lived. At first it involved her collecting magazines and taking them around to her neighbours to swap, and to read. Very quickly this expanded to include a book exchange. Not every neighbour was interested of course and some people never answered the door but increasingly people did and Alice got to know lots of people through doing this and had a role that people enjoyed, of helping cement connectedness in the street.

The neighbours would often ask her when she was coming around again next and the book exchange expanded to take in the local GP's surgery too. But after a while, Alice had to move house and so the book swap stopped. One of the neighbours kept in touch and Alice still goes back to the local pub where she used to live. This was important as the staff there had got to know her and it was one of Alice's favourite places because it had a nice sofa and good wine! Recently in her new neighbourhood Alice has started a new book club based at a local drop-in centre, where people can come along to swap books or listen to a book being read aloud.

Recognition and visibility keeps people safer than being in institutions or services

The statistics are horrendous about how many people have been hurt and abused in services and in institutions. People can be hurt anywhere of course, but making sure people are seen can ensure that they are noticed when they need help.

It's not for everyone but it is well worth considering finding places in community where people can become appreciated regulars – like pubs, cafés, hairdressers and so on. Being well and rightly connected keeps people safe, especially when they are seen as 'one of us' or 'one of ours' – where there is a sense of being a regular customer, or attendee in a group or social setting. We learnt this when Veronica's hairdresser rang to let us know that when she was supported to use the hairdresser's her experience was different depending on which member of Getta Life staff was with her. She explained that one of the staff was much more confident and relaxed in how she helped Veronica to have her hair washed and because of this Veronica had a more relaxing and enjoyable experience. As a result of this information it was possible to begin conversations with the team about the differences in how they offer assistance, and thereafter to help the staff who were not doing it so well to improve.

A similar thing happened at the pub where Neil was a regular and well-known customer. One day, the bar staff rang in to talk about one of the people who was supporting him. After a visit to the pub to talk with the bar staff there it became clear that one staff member was not supporting Neil well and we were able to take steps to change things because of the bar staff's statements.

> **Notice when new possibilities bump up against you or where there is a slight connection and increase the contact**

We had no idea when we encouraged Zara to get a rabbit what an amazing effect one small furry creature could have on the local area! We were inspired to get a rabbit because of how Zara likes to touch things and to listen to scratching sounds. Again we put two and two together and so the idea of a rabbit came into being. After some time the team noticed that the rabbit had started to spark the interest of local children. They wondered if it could help people get to know Zara too. So each day the team put the rabbit in the garden and local children would come to see it and say,

'Hello'. Sometimes the rabbit would get free and run off into nearby streets and gardens and the team spent a lot of time chasing it and bringing it home. Before long, people in the area had a conversation opener when they met Zara out and about and could ask after her rabbit, and ask if it had escaped lately. One day, a neighbour came to see if Zara would like to lend him the rabbit to breed from. At the beginning when the rabbit first arrived, no one had considered it as a method of helping to get to know Zara's neighbours. One way to look at this story is that it was simply serendipitous. The rabbit has an outdoor run in a communal garden and it became popular with the local children. It was good at escaping and so caused a lot of fun in the street when the team were trying to catch it, and Zara benefited from the increased connections and relationships that came from all of that. But to tell the story only like this misses the intentionality in the team to follow up on the connections and the interests shown by the neighbours. People bump into people all the time, whether through the mediation of a rabbit or not. It's what you do afterwards that makes the difference; the follow up, the welcome, the orchestration of other meetings, the humour and warmth of the team and friendliness in taking things a little bit further.

Finding valued roles

When Veronica first moved from living at home with her mum and dad to a residential service nearby she was very unhappy. She complained that she was being sent away. She was so unsettled that someone advised her family to move her further away, and that it would help to do so as then she couldn't keep calling them to come round! It certainly seems like strange advice to think that if you are unhappy about being sent away, you should be sent further away to make it better. For many years her mum and dad took her the long journey to the services far from home. Everyone hated it but there were no alternatives on offer. They summed this up:

> 'It was dreadful then compared to now – Veronica was often left alone for long periods, there was no kindness and no compassion. Taking her back there at the weekends, it felt like there was no way out, just crying in the car carrying her back there.'

When eventually Veronica came back to her home area she was supported to see her mum and dad and her other family in ways that would be ordinary and natural for people of her age and culture; going to visit, inviting them for tea and going away on holiday with her sister and brother-in-law, for example. Meanwhile, Veronica's dad picked Veronica up on a Saturday and she went to them for tea. Then they took her home and helped her go to bed. However, this became too much for them as Veronica's dad's health deteriorated. We talked with Veronica about how she could help and that as an adult daughter she needed to do what she could to support them. Veronica was able to accept the change, so she now visits her mum and dad and is supported to do so in her own car by her staff. Her mum and dad have been surprised and relieved and Veronica has been able to be a great support to them at a difficult time.

Being there helps others know they are here too

Sally moved into her new home and within a few months she had already become an important and perhaps essential fosterer of neighbourliness. This is poles apart from when she used to stay in a residential service where people often came and went without acknowledging her as a person or the fact that it was her home, and where there were no immediate neighbours. This bountiful change came about partly because her flat has a ground floor balcony and is part of a courtyard development. There are people who live there permanently and other flats are for short-term lets. Sally takes real pleasure in sitting and watching the world go by. Because she is so visible and so interested in other people she is naturally greeted by her neighbours as they come and go; people wave and say, 'Hi'. She knows the gardeners well now and which car is whose. So there are obvious benefits for Sally; it feels good to be welcomed, acknowledged and seen and for people to smile and chat with you. But on another level there is something important for the whole development for many of the other people who live there. They are also greeted, met, recognised, acknowledged and seen. Every interaction leads to a stronger and more cohesive local community. What looks like quite a small thing may not be a small thing at all. The role of the team is to facilitate this serendipitous role that Sally now has, to not get in the way and to make it even easier for that role to evolve. Who knows what will happen next?

Jonathan has a love of being outdoors and we thought about this when looking for things that he may like to join. He is a private man and at times finds social events a bit of a struggle, but a walking group that meets each week and a fishing club have become good places for him to be with friends.

If at first you don't succeed

Recently, Matthew's team were thinking about new experiences they could create for him. People had noticed that he sometimes stroked himself in the same way people stoke their pets. And so an idea was born to find him a pet he could stroke, but which one? Over a few weeks the team introduced Matthew to different animals. They visited a team member who had a dog and then a few other dogs were introduced to him but with no positive outcome. A lady across the street had cats so they visited and tried that. The team didn't give up there and tried rabbits. Guinea pigs followed before people stopped to take stock. No animal seemed to be of real interest. He didn't seem to like touching them. Then people thought perhaps he would like to see animals outside the house as he often liked looking out of the window. As the team kept thinking and trying out things, the conversation turned more and more to what would be really useful and meaningful for Matthew in all of this. This is a crucial part of exploring community connections and in community-building: not to stop and be disheartened when ideas don't seem to be going anywhere. What is more important is to try something, get feedback and then analyse what you have learnt.

Before long someone had the idea of getting chickens for the back garden. A little bit of networking and two chickens arrived. The team built a run for them. Matthew was interested and liked to look at them. The nagging question, 'How can we make this more useful and more meaningful?' still preyed on the team's minds and then they hit on the idea of a small business. Now he has a business as a small-scale, free-range egg farmer. From this he and his team have developed relationships with his neighbours and with other chicken experts in the local neighbourhood. It's interesting to remember that the starting point was getting animals to stroke and the end point is having a garden full of chickens, a micro-business, and many new acquaintances. What helped the team to get to this point was a committed attitude of discovery and learning, an idea to keep exploring and trying things, and questioning, what is meaningful and purposeful that could help Matthew to have a more interesting and connected life?

CHAPTER 7
Community

KEY MESSAGES

- ☑ All people need to belong somewhere, to be recognised and wanted.
- ☑ Believe in and discover people's gifts.
- ☑ The first message about community that a person should get is that they and their team are in it together.
- ☑ Discover what brings out the best in the people you support and find how to help them get more of it.
- ☑ Don't be scared about the community; the community is generally a safe place and support staff need to be brave.
- ☑ Staff and their family and friends can be a very valuable source of connection. This might be a good place to start but shouldn't be the place you finish.
- ☑ Community can be anywhere, it can evolve and strengthen from any connection with careful support.
- ☑ Give community options but never impose them.
- ☑ Believe in the value of community and the importance of feeling that you belong.
- ☑ Take as much time and thought to support people with friendships and relationships as with the rest of your work.
- ☑ Being known and being seen makes people safer.

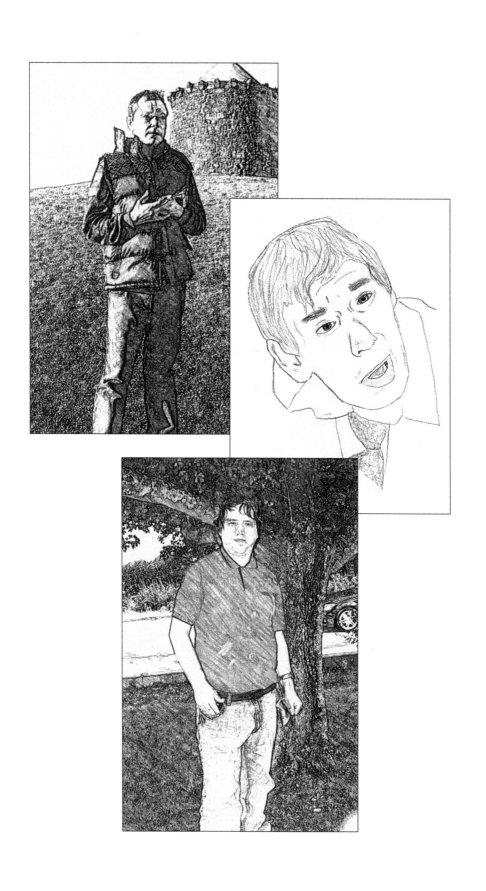

Chapter 8

Safety, Security and Healing

Written by Julie Smith of Getta Life

Before we can grow and learn, trust ourselves and others, and simply relax and enjoy ourselves, we have to feel safe. We have to trust that our safety is not fragile and feel secure in the belief that things will be all right and the people around us won't hurt us or let us down. It makes a difference today what we believe about tomorrow. When tomorrow comes it will bring its ups and downs and we need to feel that come what may we will have the support we need from those we rely on.

All too often the people we support have had experiences that have damaged their trust in others and therefore their ability to feel safe and secure. Our responsibility to those in this position is to accept that they have been hurt, and to allow them time to heal – and most importantly ensure that the support they receive from us is instrumental in that healing.

For many people healing has to be taken into account in the planning process and teams need to understand that it takes time to recover and grow even when people are living in their own homes with good support.

The things we should listen to

Understanding what the person is telling us means looking at the simple things in life and appreciating the importance in them. Take sleep, for example; going to bed and dropping off to sleep is my favourite part of the day, that brief looking back over the day, feeling that I can't do any more now and feeling secure, warm and safe. Within minutes I am asleep and remain so all night, something I completely took for granted until we started supporting people in Getta Life and I realised that how well people sleep tells us about them and how they're feeling.

When we started to support Sandra seven years ago she refused to get into bed for the first few nights in her new home. We thought it was because moving house had made her anxious and she would get into bed when she was ready. After a few days we started to think about this a bit more as there was no sign of her getting into bed. We realised that the bed was on the opposite wall to where it had been in her old house so she needed to get in on a different side; we turned the bed around and that night she got into bed. A simple thing to get right but somehow we'd missed it! It was some time before Sandra lay down on her bed; in the last place she'd lived she had always slept sitting up. One night after about twelve months she took herself to her bedroom, got into bed, covered herself with the duvet, lay down and said 'Ooh hoo', and went to sleep.

Karl used to get up at 4.00am every morning when we began to support him; he would be up at the front door with his bag wanting to go out. Gradually over time Karl has started to sleep longer and enjoy a more relaxed morning before leaving home between 9.00am and 10.00am depending on what he's doing. Most nights Karl now sleeps well and wakes up about 6.00am. He is happy to check that his team member is in their bed and wait for them to get up, rather than pulling them out of bed whatever the time. The quality of Karl's sleep is much better and his face looks significantly less stressed and worried.

Patrick has always had an irregular sleep pattern. Sometimes he sleeps really well and at other times he is up a lot of the night. Over time he has started to sleep more and be awake less, but we don't worry when he doesn't sleep now as we know it is part of his natural pattern. Patrick always sleeps with his shoes on as sometimes he needs to get up and walk about during the night. As mentioned in an earlier chapter, walking and movement is how Patrick self-soothes and manages his feelings of anxiety. It's important that he feels safe at night so keeping his shoes on makes perfect sense if you understand his level of anxiety and understand how he tries to manage this himself.

Matthew found it particularly difficult to go to bed and would get very anxious at bedtime; he would get into bed lots of times but then get up again, move the furniture around, take us to the bed, get in and then get out again, and sometimes he didn't sleep at all for several nights. There were lots of things that were very hard for Matthew that we struggled to understand properly. We asked a psychotherapist for help, and although Matthew doesn't talk her insight and understanding was invaluable. Crucially she noticed that when she spent time with him he was so vigilant that if he started to drop off to sleep he pinched himself to stay awake. Once we understood that he was frightened to go to sleep we could help to make bedtimes, bed and the bedroom a safer, more predictable place for him. We did this by agreeing in the team meeting with Matthew how people would support Matthew at bedtimes, how Matthew could let us know if it wasn't right and how we would respond. Over three years this has slowly enabled Matthew to sleep better and now his sleep pattern is largely set and he sleeps well. If there are changes to his team he doesn't sleep again until he has satisfied himself that he is safe with the new team member.

When Veronica moved into her own home for the first time, the thing she worried about most was her bed arriving on time. It looked to me like it was the presence of her bed that assured her she was staying. Veronica always wakes when her support staff open the door at her home and initially she wanted to get up immediately; it never seemed as if she was asleep or settled. Nowadays Veronica likes to have a chat with us and a cup of tea in bed before she gets up. In playful mood a pillow fight is good fun and often she will have a lie-in.

When Alice moved into her new home it was a few weeks before she made it into the bedroom. She would snooze side by side with her staff on her sofa for short periods of time day and night and would often be unsettled in the night. The team knew that Alice was learning to be in her own home for the first time and it would take her time to make sense of that. After a few weeks she would sleep some nights and not others; her staff would encourage her into the bedroom with toys she liked and cups of tea. The best thing now for Alice is breakfast in bed!

Claire found sleeping very difficult. Before moving to her own home, night-time had always been a stressful time for her. The first two nights in her own home Claire didn't sleep. On the third night she indicated to the staff that she wanted them to sleep in the bed with her; we since found out that when she was small she shared her mum's bed. Clearly the staff couldn't do this but they agreed to stay with her in the room. Claire began to settle at night and staff slept on the floor next to her bed.

Gradually the staff started to move further away and then on to the landing. We knew that in the past before Claire started to be supported by Getta Life she had been shut out of the staff's bedroom, and at times she'd got anxious as the staff did not respond to her when she needed them. Because of this we decided to take the door off the staff bedroom: a clear message that they wouldn't leave her and that she could always get to them.

It worked and the staff were able to sleep in their own beds. Eventually the door was put back on and Claire spent a long time saying goodnight to the staff after they were in bed and checking that they were there. This took Claire about eight months.

These days she goes to bed when she wants to and the staff go up when she has gone to bed. She gets up when she wants, often lies in and doesn't get disturbed if the staff get up first.

Knowing what to focus on

Eating is another simple thing that tells us a lot about how people are. Jonathan enjoys his food; however, he is a private man and has had times when he's been unhappy. When he's uncomfortable with someone he doesn't let them support him to eat; he closes his mouth tightly and moves his head. He used to live in a residential service and when I met him there were some staff who would either decide he didn't want to eat or they would try to make him. I went with him regularly to visit his mum and I observed how she supported him to eat and how much he would eat. Jonathan's mum would sit on the floor alongside him and talk with him in Polish calmly and quietly. It was clear that she cared about him and wanted to be giving him his dinner and Jonathan appeared totally happy and comfortable being given food by her.

At times when we have been supporting him he has given us concern over his eating and has lost weight. We decided in the team meeting to take our focus off whether or not Jonathan was eating and to concentrate on spending quiet time with him; reading, listening to music, going for walks; in other words, to focus on our relationship with him. We decided to give him his food wherever he seemed comfortable;

if not at the table, then on the floor where he sits or in his bed. We don't have any worries about Jonathan eating now and we let new staff know that Jonathan will eat with them when he likes them. There is a sense of pride when Jonathan eats with them for the first time.

During Jonathan's planning day we were talking about Jonathan's gifts and talents and a member of his team talked about how much of a support Jonathan had been to him during a recent lonely time in his life. He spoke of how easy Jonathan is to talk to and to confide in and also of how peaceful he is to be with. To our surprise we realised that others felt the same and we talked about sitting quietly with Jonathan and reflecting, and about the fact that when you do this you begin to feel OK about things. The planning had helped us to see Jonathan's ability to support others to discover equilibrium.

In order to notice and to understand the meaning of these small things we need to be watchful. What we notice one day needs to be considered in relation to what we notice over time.

All staff need to develop their watchfulness as they are there, day-to-day, doing the everyday things with the people they support. Being watchful means they don't miss important opportunities to understand the people they support. We often ask staff what they have noticed about the person and we talk a lot about what we see in the person's life. Watchfulness isn't about being busy, it's about spending time with the people we support in a way that fits best with them. We ensure that the staff know that it's OK to spend time with people relaxing, listening and learning, and that in fact they are expected to.

Hiding behind tasks, giving too much importance to looking busy, is talked about as a negative thing as it takes away the opportunity to connect.

It is in the reflective relationship that we heal.

SAFETY, SECURITY AND HEALING

Building trust

When we started to support Justin, it was very clear that he didn't feel safe in his own home. Justin owned his house but his support had broken down for the second time when we first met him and he had returned to live with his parents. Our aim was to help him to move back to his own home; this took some time as he only felt safe with his parents. When we first met him the only time he wasn't overwhelmed by anxiety was when he was being distracted and not with too many people. We spent time with him and tried hard to encourage him to have fun as we felt this was the key to helping Justin learn to trust us and to ease his anxiety. We engaged him in things that he found interesting; playing games, swimming, trips in the car, visits to the pub and going for walks. Over a few weeks we began to go back to Justin's house for tea before he returned to his parent's house. Justin constantly talked about where he would be sleeping and when he would be returning to his mum and dad's. We took the next step one night when Justin's parents went out. We supported him to go to his regular club where he's been going for years and which he loves, and then we went back to his own house to sleep, returning to his parents' home the next morning. This was a number of years ago and Justin now lives back in his own home. He visits his parents on Sundays, stays the night and returns to his own home on Mondays. Justin is living fully in his own house now and sees it as home; he watches TV, uses his computer, plays games, helps with housework, sleeps very well and is living again. There are still times when he gets very anxious but he is learning to tell us before he gets lost in it and asking us to help him stay in control until the feeling has passed.

Justin's parents have been invaluable in helping us to learn how to support Justin. When things have gone wrong, when people have been hurt, when trust has been broken, they have never wavered in their belief in Justin and in their willingness to assist us and help us to puzzle out what is happening. We have learnt that it doesn't work to have anxious staff supporting someone who is already highly anxious; then there's too much anxiety in one place and it overwhelms Justin. Some staff in Justin's team have found this difficult to admit and to do what's right for Justin. His story also illustrates how it doesn't work to not listen to what family tell us; everything that Justin's parents have told us has been right.

If a team member is having a tough time this is enough to tip Justin's anxiety as he feels less safe. Recently the team manager was very anxious about his wife who was in hospital; this meant Justin had a big wobble: too much anxiety in one place again. Justin's family suggested we ask Justin to help us when we are struggling. Justin has the capacity to support us, and this also helps him to understand why things may feel a bit different at times.

Justin likes to plan his day each morning with the two people who will support him that day; he then reminds us of the plan. Too many shift changes make Justin anxious and spoil the day as he gets stuck worrying about who is coming next, so we only change staff once a day now, in the mornings, and this has made it much more predictable for Justin. I have learnt not to over-react when things go wrong, accept that most things can be sorted out when they happen and to believe in Justin's ability to grow and develop better coping strategies. A strong, calm team manager who comes over as safe and dependable is essential, as are team members who accept that at times it may go wrong but who trust that things will go well again.

When Rebecca moved to her new home she had to get to know three new staff who made up her new team. Rebecca uses routines and familiarity to help her feel safe, and so the new staff knew that for a while Rebecca would be anxious. Letting Rebecca take the lead and show us what she was comfortable with has allowed her to quickly become confident with us. This meant listening carefully and being happy to listen over and over again. It meant not putting pressure on

Rebecca to do things differently but letting her know she could. We worked out when to give up an idea, and when to try again. Her home is lovely and it's satisfying to see how confident she has become there. Over a few months we have seen her face change as she has relaxed; she has begun to take an interest in her appearance, going to the hairdresser's and wearing make-up. She has allowed herself to be beautiful and is enjoying the compliments this brings. We have discovered her very funny sense of humour and seen her out and about on picnics, wearing varied outfits; these little things tell us we're on the right track. Today I rang Rebecca to ask how she was; she said she was OK. I asked her how her staff were; '*We are happy in my home*', she replied. That says it all!

One of the things that Claire finds hard is the changing over of staff. She likes to be sure who is on the sleep-in and this often causes her anxiety until the team member who will be sleeping in arrives. There are times when she has two staff with her for certain things she wants to do, but having two staff with her at home is also stressful for her. We tried several rotas and eventually settled for one that means the team member who arrives in the morning stays with her for the whole day and sleeps in. This ensures that Claire is not anticipating a change-over once she's ready to go out and about. Both staff arrive in the morning and one leaves when Claire is home for the evening. Claire doesn't get anxious when staff leave, so this works well for her.

We have also tried lots of ways to do the team meeting so that Claire can be a part of it. We know that in the past, pre-Getta Life, staff excluded her from meetings and she has consequently been anxious about them, especially because a lot of what was said in meetings about Claire was negative and restrictive.

We are working to understand more about how to support Claire in her meetings. We have things to do, such as makeovers, drawing or craft work. We are sitting differently as we have decided that by having the dining chairs in the lounge it looks like a meeting and sets it aside from other times when we are all together, such as parties. We talk positively even about the difficult stuff. When Claire shows us she has had enough we let her know that we understand and we draw to a close. Sometimes we meet in the pub instead of her home.

Be honest, don't make false promises and know when to say sorry

---

Trust is a fragile thing and to build it takes time and a consciousness of what we are doing.

It is crucial that in our work we do what we say we will and that we don't make false promises or say things that are untrue. This may sound obvious but we know that in the past people have been let down and lied to, so any repetition of that from us would be compounding the hurt.

Be prepared to say sorry: it's human to make mistakes and in all relationships there will be times when apologies are needed. We must therefore acknowledge when things go wrong and say sorry, and not only this, we must then work to ensure that the same thing doesn't happen again, otherwise the apology is meaningless.

We explain to all staff the abuses of the past and how they have shaped the person they know today. In respecting this we can understand the things that people do and therefore respond in sensitive and healing ways.

We work to build strong and real relationships with the people we support, ensuring that staff know that is their work. They plan for fun and for joy as well as for quiet times of reflection together and for relaxation.

We take small steps together as we spend time with each other day by day. We stick with people when things are tough and face adversity shoulder to shoulder. Most importantly we listen and let people be themselves.

Employing the right people

Getting the right team members around the person is also important. In recruiting we look for staff with the right skills for the person. For example, for Justin we know that anxious staff won't work. There are people who need nurturing staff and there are staff who nurture well; there are people who need assertive staff and staff who fill this need. Both these characteristics can contribute to people feeling secure, albeit in different ways. Understanding this allows us to put in place the right team around each person we support.

We expect staff to work rotas that suit the person they are supporting; for example Karl usually gets up at 6.30am so we ensure the staff work around his needs. We talk about why this is important, ensuring we meet the needs of the people we support while being as flexible as possible with regard to staff needs.

Being brave

We can't consider safety without talking about risk. Risk has become a big factor in how services make their decisions and so it is important, if people are to develop and we are to continue to make discoveries, that we maintain a balanced view and response to risk.

It is common for us to ask staff to be brave; this allows the people we support to have wider experiences.

A family member spoke of the way we consider risk. She said, *'The risk assessments are used to enable people to achieve their wishes and desires. It's a process of considering the question "How can we?", rather than the reasons not to do something'*.

Another way to keep risk in perspective is to consider the risk of not doing something alongside the risk of doing it.

For Neil, this has arisen about his health. He is an adventurous young man, his health is very fragile, and it's common for him to become very ill very quickly. It would be easy to be protective and in doing so restrict him. Part of the way we support Neil is to consider what we call health versus happiness, thinking about each day and ensuring that it's as good as it can be based on his health in the here and now.

This allows Neil to do everything he would want to and to live life to the full at the times that he can; we ensure that no period of good health is wasted.

Neil has been swimming, rock climbing, canoeing, to the theatre, and on several holidays. He has experienced different weathers and stayed out late, he has taken long journeys and has been tired out. We see being tired as a positive thing.

We start from the view that most folk are well-intentioned. It's important that we're not suspicious of the outside world, that we embrace it as the opportunity to meet new people and in doing so open ourselves to possible new relationships. We teach the teams to value community places and to notice those they come across who show an interest and who the person they support likes. These are the opportunities they have to support the person to become more connected. We believe that genuine connections help people stay safe. The more people there are with a genuine interest in you, and the more friends you have in your life, then the more you are looked out for.

If our teams follow this principle then the people we support become braver in the world after years of being shut away.

Matthew found getting out of his house really hard when he first moved into his home. The team spent two or three years working to gain his trust. They did this by doing nice things with him at home and by respecting his communication; in particular recognising how he said no and how he was feeling. We never gave up thinking that one day he would make it and we all recognised that it was important to keep believing. The real risk that we saw was in us accepting that the community was out of bounds for Matthew. Gradually he started venturing out, but this was still hard for him and the way he would tell us he was feeling unsafe was undignified for him and potentially embarrassing for the public and for support staff.

In the team meetings we talked a lot about what was the worst thing that could happen. We knew and accepted that this was to be embarrassed; we knew that no one would actually get hurt. It was important that the staff felt that they would be supported at the times when it went wrong. One practical measure we took was to carry a card that explained a little of what was happening and offered reassurance and a contact number; this could be passed to members of the public when things got uncomfortable. These steps were taken at Matthew's pace and within the context of safe relationships and have given Matthew his life back – these days you'd be lucky to find him in!

When there is a risk that is real we have to hold true to the same beliefs and to ensure that our response is appropriate and doesn't become excessive due to the anxiety of ourselves or others. For Claire there had been lots of restrictions; these had come about due to some rare yet real risks. These restrictions in our view were not necessary or fair, but had been imposed due to the anxiety of some of the professionals involved. It seemed as though little value was given to Claire's life experiences or to her right to a home and to a community life; very little thought was given to how to support her to develop. Our challenge was to ensure that Claire could still have a great life and to work with the multi-disciplinary team to gradually get them to minimise the restrictions. The importance of Claire's family and friends in this can't be over-emphasised. They were the ones who really *cared* that the restrictions were just. They were the people who properly knew her, and their involvement meant that the professionals who were making the decisions could never lose sight of who Claire is and the impact their decisions would have on her. The other important aspect of getting this right was again our willingness to accept a risk that ensured that Claire had opportunities to take part in the community.

Acknowledging people's pasts and believing people can heal

Healing and safety are precarious things in life. They are easily compromised and the impact of feeling unsafe or of being hurt can be devastating to people, and so they are things that need to be thought about and nurtured. This is done through knowing and holding in our mind the abuses and hurts that people have experienced. Believing that time and time again services have got it wrong and people have been hurt. Accepting that this is the reason that things are as they are today and being very clear that it isn't the person's fault. This leads us to teach staff and others around the person that society has in the past treated people badly. As we are all part of that society each one of us can be part of putting it right.

Alongside this there is a belief that people can heal; it's just as harmful to see a person only as a victim and not in other roles. We need to acknowledge that healing is an on-going thing and that people will heal in their own time once they begin to feel safe. Healing isn't something we can do to another; our role is to provide the safety and happiness that allows the person to heal him or herself.

This safety and happiness has to be there for a long time before the healing begins, and for the healing to continue the safety and happiness must also continue. Thinking carefully if things need to change; for example if a member of staff is leaving, talking this through with the person, explaining change, apologising where appropriate and keeping as consistent as possible are all important. Listening to the things that people are telling us and paying attention to the things that people do is our only way of working out how it is for them. We must be prepared to hear what we don't want to and what we don't understand.

To support healing, hope and encouragement is needed because when healing is slow teams can lose heart. Hope comes from understanding the person's story, but more importantly from the relationships and the ability to notice and celebrate small steps. It comes from knowing that there is a journey to take together over time and that others have made this journey.

When we first began to support Claire she had been hurt by a member of staff at the service where she had been living. The person who had hurt her was found guilty and fined; it was so good to be able to tell Claire that she'd had justice. Some time after, we recruited a new member of staff and she wasn't working in the way we wanted her to. Another member of staff, Debbie, saw her getting cross and shouting and rightly sent her home. This member of staff wasn't allowed to return to work and was dismissed from Getta Life.

It was so important that Claire saw Debbie, her support staff, protect her from the member of staff who was shouting and that I was able to say sorry it had happened and tell Claire that the member of staff would not come back, to her home or to Getta Life.

At the time, Bernadetha was working with Claire and was also reasonably new; when Claire was upset or cross she sometimes told us this by hurting others. She had hurt Bernadetha a few times and Bernadetha was having a struggle to stay. I talked a lot with Bernadetha about how important she would be to Claire's healing if she could stick with it for a while and show Claire that she would be there for her whatever. Bernadetha needed courage and encouragement. Four years on, Bernadetha still works with Claire and since they built their relationship Claire has been able to let new staff into her life without upset and without hurting them.

Thinking about families

We must work with the supported person's family to understand more of their story and recognise the important bond between family and friends as central to our understanding of the person. All of these things ensure that we think through how best to support the person in a purposeful way; we must ask ourselves if what we propose makes sense for the person, given their story.

Supporting families to heal and to re-form the relationships they have with their family member comes as the person heals. Where families have been the voice and the champion for many years, it can be a hard thing to go back to being a mum, dad, sister or brother. Talking things through, and finding ways to support the person to give back, help develop two-way relationships that are more equal and less stressful.

Risk is another aspect of healing and safety. Achieving the right balance between risk-taking and safety is part of the way that healing is nurtured, whereas protection can lead to hurt and to fear.

Paramount, and as previously mentioned, we must not be suspicious of the world. People are safer when they are connected to and known by people who are not paid staff. The people we support grow and heal as a result of being seen as part of society and being given the opportunity to contribute to it.

Families have often earned reputations that originate from earlier conflicts with professionals over what is right for their family member. When we listen to their stories, and hear what is being said without prejudging them by listening to the reputation, then we find that we can work together to get it right for the person, and as a result relationships heal.

Claire's sisters had always been strong for her. There had been many times when she had been treated badly by services and they'd stood up for her. They wanted Claire to have her own home and to be supported in a true person-centred way. However, Claire was viewed by services as challenging, and they responded to her from this viewpoint. This resulted in her life being restricted by risk assessments and in everything being controlled around her. There were lots of rules that she was made to live by that only served to increase her need to be challenging in a bid to gain some control. Lots of past actions towards her made no sense at all and many times support had gone wrong. Eventually her sisters secured an individual budget and Claire moved into her own home supported by Getta Life. Over time Claire has changed how she communicates. Talking and showing us more and more, she makes her own choices and is in control of how things happen in her home. The challenging behaviours that in the past had earned her a label have all but gone and she listens, responds, and knows that waiting is OK because people do what they say. At Claire's last planning day we talked with her family about getting back to being sisters and since then Claire has picked them up for nights out. She's been to the pub with them, to the theatre and swimming. When they spend time together now, it's about having a good time.

Our work with her sisters is a partnership, working together through any worries or ideas we have. Incidentally, it was their idea to take the door off the spare bedroom used for staff sleep-ins.

When we started to work with Justin, the provider service had given notice. Justin had his own home but was living with his family as his support had completely broken down. Justin's family had a reputation, they were often blamed when Justin was struggling and they were seen as interfering because they'd pop in and notice things and make suggestions. Understandably when we first met them they weren't convinced that what we said could be true. We were aware that it would take time for us to gain their trust and respect and that we shouldn't expect that to come easily. We know that when we work with a person we work with their family and that listening, honesty, and seeing things through are key. One of the things that Justin's family see now is that we like Justin, and we don't think he should change or that he or his family are a problem. We're discovering with them the things that work well for Justin so that he can keep his anxiety at a manageable level. We talk to them when there have been difficulties, not with the expectation that they should solve them or with any feeling that they are responsible, but to get their insight as to what may be wrong and how best to respond. There is a real sense of partnership in the relationship that staff have with Justin's mum and dad that has allowed them to feel positive about Justin's future and to relax about him in a way they've not been able to before.

Neil's health is often compromised and it's crucial that he receives the correct medical help quickly should he become unwell, as he gets seriously ill quickly. Neil's grandparents, who brought him up from a small boy, often found themselves having to push doctors to treat him promptly and be vigilant on his behalf that the care was right. It was a very hard decision for them to support Neil to leave home and to lead an independent life, yet they knew they were limiting him because his physical care was getting harder as he grew and they were finding it difficult to summon the energy to take him out and about as much as they wanted to. They also knew he didn't like attending day care and that he went there to please them, not for himself.

For a long time after Neil moved out they worried. They worried about everything but particularly whether the staff would talk to him and whether they would notice quickly enough when he was ill. There was nothing we could do to reassure them except to listen and make sure we got it right. It was especially difficult for them each time staff changed – and for some time after Neil moved into his house supported by Getta Life this happened too regularly for various reasons. Each time we had new staff we told Neil's grandparents why and we tried to help them to get to know the new person. We always invite all the team to Neil's circle meeting and planning days as we know that his family are happier the more they see and familiarise themselves with the people who support Neil. We've talked a lot with them about how we induct people and they have suggested that this is always done by Godfrey, one of our support staff and someone they see as very thorough.

A supported person's family often holds the key to understanding the person and their knowledge of the person's past is invaluable. When we are stuck we ask them to help and they always have ideas and advice that works. Little things make sense the more you know. When we first met Alice's sister she spoke about her mum and how the kitchen was the hub of the house; she told us that their mum always had a kettle on the boil, on a low whistle so that anyone who arrived could get a cup of tea. As she spoke I smiled – one of the things Alice has always done since I met her was to take me to the kettle! I knew that she was telling me she wanted a cup of tea, but it wasn't until I heard Betty talk that I realised how important it was for me to get the response right. In doing this small thing right I was confirming and honouring Alice's sense of home.

Creating the right conditions

Many of the people we support have had periods of bad health, often as a consequence of their lives in institutions. At separate times four of the people we support have become unwell with pneumonia. On each occasion we were told by the medical staff that they would most likely not recover. Each person made a full recovery and we began to reflect on what had happened and what was in place to give people the best possible outcome.

We believe many factors contributed to this:

- Benefiting from good support where people are encouraged to be healthy and therefore have a better starting place for recovery.

- Being really loved and connected as well as having a sense of purpose and a meaningful life that gives people the will to live.

- Being supported by authentic people who genuinely care as well as working with family and friends to be powerful advocates.

- Being able to call upon staff who are comfortable with helping outsiders (in this case medical professionals) to see the person and their value, especially as it's easy for medical staff to dismiss people with learning difficulties – they often see them as uncooperative when needing medical treatment, and they can also struggle with how to assess consent.

We've received supportive feedback from professionals regarding our practices. A doctor supporting Alice said, *'She got better because you are caring for her so well.'* The community nurse for Neil said his care at Getta Life had continued the dedicated support of his family which kept him well. A paramedic commented to a member of staff, *'Well done, you acted so promptly you saved his life'*.

We also acknowledge that anxiety can be a debilitating feeling especially when someone is away from their own territory. It's important to know people well enough to be able to help medical staff know when it is detrimental for someone to be in hospital. It requires especially good GP support to ensure someone can be treated effectively at home, and these relationships have to be built and worked on, not just at the point when someone becomes ill.

Supporting good health

Roy had been living in a specialist residential service for people with epilepsy when I met him. He was very unhappy, anxious about everything and was often told he was demanding too much if he wanted to go out to the local shop to spend a bit of his money.

Most of his time was spent in one side room, on his bed watching TV, and he had become very routine-focused. Roy was seen as uncooperative and as confrontational. He often wouldn't wear his protective helmet or take his medication and he denied that he had seizures. As a result of these fits he was often injured, and had cut his head and broken his nose on several occasions.

When Roy moved to his flat he had a small team of three people who got to know him very well and talked with both respect and a focus on negotiation and equality, not control. Over time, the difference we've seen in Roy is amazing. He has a full and active life and is out every day enjoying friendships and relationships, football, snooker at the club where he is a member, bowling, sailing, carriage-riding, college and a job. He wears his helmet reliably and asks for his medication. It's clear from talking to Roy that he feels completely in control of his life and in tune and happy with his team. The incidence of injury has reduced and although he does still suffer injuries at times his ability to cope with the need to go to hospital and let people help him is much improved. Roy will discuss his seizures with the doctors and his team, and will talk to us comfortably about his safety. On one occasion his team all sat together and told each other the rules they have for their own safety and Roy set his own rules for staying safe during his seizures.

The importance of knowing you are cared for

Neil has many health frailties and as a result has been admitted a few times to hospital with pneumonia. On one occasion he was extremely poorly and was admitted and treated in ITU. It was terribly sad to see him so ill and to know that he might not recover.

What was clear was how much Neil was loved. Many people visited and there was constantly someone at his side. People sat and talked to him about his life and the things he could do and achieve. Knowing he was loved and that he had a life he enjoyed appeared to give him a will to live that was strong enough to beat the odds and enable him to recover.

Recently Alice has had two episodes of pneumonia in quick succession, both resulting in hospital stays. Alice had never been ill before, never been in hospital, and so she was really scared.

Her team stayed with her twenty-four hours a day, offering her good care and reassurance. They were able to help the doctors and nurses understand her and know her needs and made the stay in hospital bearable. It was important that her team kept telling Alice where she was and that they were with her.

At one point Alice had a panic attack during the night and her staff were there to tell the doctor what was normal and what was new. Between the doctor and the support staff they were able to help Alice relax.

Alice was clear that she was valued, loved and cared for. Her sister Betty, friend Wyn and boyfriend Matthew visited regularly. I felt that having the right people around her played a big part in ensuring Alice's recovery.

Not getting caught by labels and expectations

When people have mental health issues as well as learning difficulties it requires a lot of careful thought and observation to work out what we can do to support each part of the person's life.

Following the closure of the long-stay institutions in line with the community living programme of the 1980s, Terry moved in with a foster carer under the adult placement scheme. Unfortunately following the sudden death of his foster carer he had to move into residential provision. When we first met Terry he was living in a long-stay hospital, as his service provider had given him notice following the collapse of a ceiling after he'd blocked a toilet. Terry was labelled as obsessive, and known to have a compulsion for blocking toilets. This was controlled in the hospital by restrictions on everyone's access to toilet paper. He had few personal belongings and every time we saw him he would say his case was packed. He was desperate to leave the hospital. His face was red and sore where he frequently and anxiously washed it and he looked stressed and strained.

Eventually Terry moved back to his home town where we now support him in his own ground floor flat. It quickly became clear to us that he has many so-called compulsions;

he regularly threw away tea bags, sugar and milk so he could go to the shop and buy more. While shopping he would insist on buying hats, sunglasses or bangles – whatever was the particular passion of the week. Terry spent long periods of time in the toilet and at first he would block it on occasions. The team quickly realised that if there were lots of toilet rolls in the bathroom Terry was less anxious. We reflected on his other needs for collecting and hoarding. He had huge amounts of papers, folders and cuttings in his bedroom, all over the floor and in his drawers. He also prefers his clothes hidden under or behind the bed; whenever they are hung in the wardrobe or put away in drawers he immediately takes them out and puts them back where he wants them. Terry seems to have a deep need to be able to see all his belongings and possessions; he can't tolerate them being put away. We began to learn that if we rigidly control his needs this makes him highly anxious, and this anxiety results in him being unable to join in any activities.

Over time Terry has become funny, warm and appreciative of his team. His trust and faith in his team has developed and improved and the quality and depth of the relationship he has with them is impressive, based as it is on mutual respect and shared fun. Terry is cheeky and very clear if he is unhappy or displeased with anyone. As a team we have worked gently with Terry to try and put some parameters around his collections while ensuring he is able to do what he needs to feel emotionally secure. For example, while recognising that by most people's standards Terry's bedroom is chaotic, crammed full and incredibly messy we have worked with him to enable him to keep it how he wants without imposing too much order. The mutually understood bottom line is that when his room becomes a hazard to him then the whole team help to clear it to a safe level again. We have learnt that if we clear it out completely Terry feels deeply distressed. Terry accepts this support because he knows he will be able to keep it how it feels OK to him and that he can rebuild his collections again.

The rest of Terry's life is now much richer: he undertakes some voluntary work in a café; he has reconnected with his family and has made many friends. Terry loves having his own home and takes great pride in saying, *'this is mine'*. Terry's speech is much clearer and he talks all the time. Terry is well known in his town and is always meeting people he knows. Terry goes to college and is charismatic and engaging. His physical health has improved, his skin is clear, he looks younger and most importantly he is happy and proud of who he is.

Knowing when to get professional help

There are times when people need professional help. Getting the right help at the right time is crucial for healing. We need to notice when people have got stuck and may need help to move forward; we also need to notice patterns in people's communication that may be telling us of their distress. For some people there are times when their mental health may need some support from the mental health professionals.

When we met Zara she suffered from extreme changes of mood; these often caused her to be distressed for long periods of time and it was believed this was simply how Zara was. This meant that the staff at the residential service where she was living hadn't considered that this may be a mental health issue and therefore hadn't got her any help.

After Zara moved to be supported by Getta Life, the mood changes didn't lessen so we asked for a referral to a psychiatrist. Some medication was recommended and over a period of time her mood changes ameliorated. They still happen but the periods of distress are very short-lived and we have found that a bath at these times will help her to keep calm.

Once Zara was settled we asked for the medication to be stopped, but this badly affected Zara and she had to start re-taking it. It was obvious that the mood changes are due to some underlying mental health issues.

Just recently Zara's psychiatrist has reduced the medication again and she is doing well. Working together in this way we have supported Zara to manage her mental health more effectively.

The way we use advice from other professionals has to hold true to the person-centred values we hold. The same piece of advice may be right for one person and not another. The physiotherapist had advised us to hold toys that Sandra would want to take from us up in the air above her head and to the front of her. This encourages her to straighten up and helps her scoliosis. For Sandra this was right.

We received the same advice regarding Jonathan; we were also asked to try talking to him and supporting him to eat with our faces higher than his; however, for him it was wrong. Jonathan is most comfortable on the floor and when we first knew him he had been so disconnected by the services he had received he would turn his back if you tried to see his face. It has taken many years for Jonathan to be comfortable with face-to-face contact and we feel honoured that he now holds his face to ours if we sit alongside him at his level. The healing that came with beginning to trust again and reconnect with people was more important than the physiotherapy. We needed to find other ways to support Jonathan in stretching himself.

There was a time when we knew that Karl was different from before. He was making a noise that he hadn't made formerly; he would make the noise for long periods of time and seemed unable to focus on anything else. He would become restless, was sweating and did not eat. We supported him to see a consultant psychiatrist several times before he suggested an investigative ECG. This showed Karl had epileptic activity happening all the time. Once the medication was prescribed Karl became much more settled and has stopped making this different noise.

CHAPTER 8

Safety, Security and Healing

KEY MESSAGES

- ☑ Don't make the person into someone who is only seen as a victim.
- ☑ Don't expect things to happen quickly.
- ☑ Look at the risk of not doing something as well as the risk of doing something.
- ☑ Ensure people are talked about positively.
- ☑ Know when to get professional help and to spot who's helpful.
- ☑ Ask the family to help find the answer.
- ☑ We should never think we can heal someone; we can set the right conditions, we can be supportive, but people heal themselves.
- ☑ Always acknowledge someone's past, especially if they have been hurt by institutions or systems.

Chapter 9

Celebration and Belonging

Written by Sue Deeley of Getta Life

*'Small, ordinary things need to be celebrated
to show how wonderful they actually are'*
– a circle member

Why is celebration important? Everyone loves to be made aware of their value, to be recognised. It's important to take time to reflect and to show that we care and have thought for what others contribute. People are most happy about themselves when they feel they are properly seen, valued, esteemed and liked. We believe that organisations need to consciously work to establish these feelings in everyone; the people supported, their families, their friends and the support staff. This approach will foster a strong organisation which is sustainable, becoming a great place to live and work and creating a sense of togetherness. It gives rise to a culture where people feel they belong; that they are welcome, respected and treated with dignity. In turn this nurtures rewarding lives for those people associated with them, including their staff. A sense of safety emerges and the right conditions arise to support personal growth and change. All this flourishes where there's an ethos of working hard in tandem with providing flexibility to support staff and encouraging their personal growth and professional development. (It isn't a coincidence that a lot of people working for support organisations are also learning and studying.) The most significant result is that the people at the centre of our work receive a more insightful style of support.

There are many different ways and opportunities to pay tribute to people, to honour and celebrate their feelings, their progress, their growth, their communication and their joy. This tribute needs to be offered over and over again in different ways making the experience powerful and felt in ways that will stay with the recipient for a long time. For people to be able to recover from past hurts and lack of value they have to hear the opposite many times before a better view of themselves can be internalised. An intentional spin-off from positive reputation-building is that the support staff always show belief in the people they work alongside, continually offering positive messages of worth. If there is a sincere belief in and liking for the people you support you will model this delight to everyone you meet. This way of being naturally generates intrigue and curiosity in other people and leads to them wanting to get to know the supported person better.

Many people receiving support have not experienced being valued or being viewed as successful or competent. The nature of the experience of having a learning difficulty means much of the world sees that person in reverse; as incompetent, stupid and worthless. The result is very poor self-esteem and consequent invisibility. It also gives rise to derogatory labels which are often attached to the person for their whole life.

People will have often internalised this devaluation and believe themselves to be worthless. Regular planned appreciation and honouring of the person is the antidote, helping them to cast off their role and take on a different view of themselves. You can't easily change the world's view of people but you can help people to start to believe in themselves and be proud of their achievements, and make sure you regularly celebrate people's accomplishments. This is magic medicine: free, not hard to do, and has an immeasurable, positive effect on people's self-esteem.

One way that we at Getta Life achieve this includes offering a gifts statement as part of the person-centred plan. This could be poster-size featuring fabulous photos of the person, prominently displayed somewhere in the person's home so they are regularly visually prompted about their gifts and dreams. Each year these statements can be re-visited, getting bigger as you discover more about the person, their talents and abilities. No one can have too much praise or celebration and once it becomes part of an organisation's culture it is life-changing for all involved. You can share stories of successes with people's families, friends, social workers and the wider community as a way of helping the person to be appreciated in a different way.

Another important message is that all of us are great as we are. The human condition is such that we all have flaws and blind spots and these we can improve, and equally we all have good sides to ourselves which need to be remembered and alluded to. We believe that people can all grow and change but it's important that people do this in a way that's right for them, and when they feel ready. We nurture the person, encourage and support them and give them the space to change if they want to. We work especially hard not to give people any indication that they're not good enough or not OK as they are. In our opinion people can only change themselves, and support services expend huge amounts of time and energy trying to impose on or force changes from people and rarely succeed.

We deem it important to have at least one event a year where everyone in the organisation gets together and celebrates achievements and has fun. Our ways of acknowledging accomplishments or encouraging fun have included a photo exhibition, an Oscars Night, a *Dragons' Den* day, posh picnics, a good health day, rounders, cricket and storytelling. Everyone who is supported by Getta Life, their families and friends and the staff are included in these events. They create lots of excitement, are much anticipated and an important part of the glue that holds our organisation together. This practice of celebration, noticing and acknowledging people's progress and gifts is cascaded throughout the organisation in the men's groups, women's groups, team meetings, supervisions and, as previously mentioned, the person-centred planning days. This approach not only instils a sense of pride in belonging to something that is achieving so much, it also encourages everyone's involvement and means people want to be part of it, which in turn enhances the sense of belonging that everybody feels.

The families of the people we support often comment on the sense of belonging that they believe their relative feels; they also talk about their own sense of belonging. Some examples include Neil's grandparents talking about the organisation providing them with a social life; not just at the celebratory events, but at Neil's circle meetings – and other shared outings and excursions with Neil, including trips to the theatre. Claire and her sister going on a girls' night out with some of her support team. Sandra being supported to go on holiday with her mum every year. Sarah's circle feeling both proud to be part of her life and proud that they have supported Sarah to grow to be the person she is.

Acceptance

Patrick and Matthew live separately in a house split into two. A while ago they hosted a barbeque to get to know their neighbours as they were ready to make some connections and reach out. After careful consideration we decided that sharing their garden space with visitors was the best option. We believed they could both manage this and knew they could always draw back to their homes if need be.

Matthew and Patrick were both relaxed with the four neighbours who came, sitting with them, listening, smiling and enjoying the food. Patrick had several plates of food, each of which he tipped on to his lap and ate with his fingers. John, who was supporting Patrick, calmly helped him to clean his hands and trousers. I watched the neighbours see this and accept it as John beautifully modelled complete acceptance.

Two of the people we support, Angela and Zara, are often more comfortable when they take their shoes off; this has been a lifelong trait. Both women are in their fifties and we guess they'll have had lots of instruction about wearing shoes. We gently try to get them to wear shoes when they are outside for obvious reasons but feel that it's not important indoors. Angela joined a cookery class at the local college. While at college she was using her wheelchair, and on arrival she would take her shoes off, as she likes to hold them by her side in the wheelchair. It was almost two whole terms before the tutor stopped fretting about Angela not wearing her shoes and began to appreciate Angela for her unique gifts and talents. Then of course Angela began to make great progress on the course and participated much more when the focus was not on her shoes. Zara joined a floristry group, and was asked to leave because she didn't keep her shoes on and didn't sit down all of the time. It took a lot of challenges and modelling from us to show that Zara is able to participate in her own way and that she has a right to be there. Education is for all; there isn't anyone who can't learn and we all learn best when we are ourselves.

Honour absolutely everything – even the small things

Things that could be deemed as little but are big for the people supported are honoured with them and across the organisation. For example, we were all excited when Alice went into her garden for the first time to sit with her newly acquired chickens, and when she got back into her bath having healed from a broken ankle. We were all excited when she got her first big order for balloons – the result of a *Dragons' Den* money-making idea where she would supply helium balloons for any Getta Life party and occasionally external customers.

Rebecca's team celebrated when she wore white trousers for the first time, having previously only ever worn black, and when we discovered how much she likes picnics and how relaxed she is when she's out and about. And we were extremely excited about her growing friendship with Claire who is a superb role model.

Rebecca looked forward to her mum and dad's thirtieth wedding anniversary party. Since moving to her own home she had struggled with family events, as excitement increased her anxiety. Everyone was surprised and pleased when she stayed at the party for four hours. She appeared to have a fantastic time with all her family and seemed able to relax, with her support staff staying all the time to assist her in feeling safe and supported.

Philip's team acknowledged and celebrated how much more he is laughing and enjoying life these days and how happy he seems. People tell him they have noticed this and thank him in the team meetings for sharing his happiness and laughter with us.

Karl's team celebrated his developing relationship with Zara, helping him to think of things they might do together and supporting him to be thoughtful and considerate in their growing romance. It's so exciting to see this side of Karl developing where he can consider someone else, and gets bashful yet animated by someone else's presence. We also celebrated the greetings Karl now gets from his neighbours and the acknowledgement of his place in his street.

Justin's team are pleased that he will often ask them to look after his glasses rather than breaking them when he loses control, which used to be his pattern. Now he will tell us he's not OK before he loses control and can sometimes take himself off to get some space and calm himself when he is getting very anxious. Justin's team often remind him of how good this is and how much it helps us to get it right for him when he assists us in this way.

Matthew's team were very excited about how much he enjoys his chickens, going into the garden to feed them each day, collecting the eggs and spending time sitting in the chicken run just watching them. They're also pleased about him carrying his laundry basket from the garden back upstairs to his flat; small things maybe, but significant, exciting and cause for celebration.

Star letters

Every month we think about any stars within Getta Life; those people who have done something special or particularly well. The managers write a thank you letter to those people to recognise their achievement. Star letters can be sent to the people supported, their family, friends, staff and colleagues from other organisations. People love to receive them; often staff will send a text to say, 'Thank you' and acknowledge how proud they are to be a recipient.

For example, we wrote to Minnie's brother to thank him for all of the help and support he gave us when we were helping Minnie to move into her home. He is a wonderful brother and works very hard to support his sister and her staff team; it was important to thank him and show we appreciate how well he works in partnership with us.

Likewise I wrote to Matthew, and to Ken on his support staff, to tell them how excited I was to see Matthew at the bowling alley in Coventry with the men's group. I was moved to tears to see Matthew playing confidently, taking his turn, knowing he got two throws each go, staying right until the end of the game, remaining dressed throughout and using the toilet at the bowling alley, all of which seemed completely natural. Knowing Matthew's journey and some of his story this is the equivalent of me running a marathon in the desert! This was such an incredible achievement; an epic journey, from being stuck on his sofa to being able to take part in an ordinary everyday activity in the community.

Reflection – noticing growth, commenting and celebrating achievements

Reflection is a big part of the role of all support staff and you can only celebrate progress if you see it. By asking everyone what they have noticed about the person they are supporting, how their relationship is and what are they doing together ensures this. Likewise this practice informs discussions in team meetings and supervision. Often in team meetings one person will say, *'This has been happening when I'm here, is it the same for you?'*. For example, Ken talked about how Matthew had wanted to go to bed earlier than normal and asked colleagues in the team meeting if they'd found the same thing. There was a feeling of satisfaction once everyone on the team realised that Matthew must be very relaxed if he is happy to sleep more; he used to be too hyper-vigilant to enjoy going to sleep and as he is more active now it would be normal for him to be more tired. So as a result of this reflection, lots of positive feedback was acquired and information confirmed, all from a simple observation.

You can notice small changes in the person and make slight adjustments to their support in response, and then wait to see if the adjustment works and what happens as a result. For example; we knew that Patrick liked flowers because he would look at them closely, allow them to be on the table or other surfaces in his home and sometimes smell them. However, he constantly emptied the water out of the vase down the sink and the flowers got damaged in the process. We talked about this at a team meeting and decided to try a ceramic vase rather than a glass one, so that Patrick couldn't see the water in it – and it worked. We know that when Patrick feels anxious he is compelled to empty things where he can see liquid in them, such as milk cartons, juice bottles and clear jugs. Patrick now buys flowers each week and leaves them in the vase; we feel this is an achievement because we have helped him to have something he takes pleasure in without causing him stress. A small thing, perhaps, but well worth celebrating.

We hadn't been supporting Rebecca very long when Agnes, her team manager, told me that all Rebecca wanted was to be heard. Rebecca repeated the same things over and over and it was often difficult to get her to focus on anything other than her concern at that time. Rebecca would talk over any conversation we were having and was unable to answer questions at these times. I listened to Agnes describe how she helped Rebecca on these occasions, by sitting quietly and waiting for Rebecca to sit with her. Agnes tells Rebecca that she understands that things are not OK for her at that moment and she offers her sympathy. She lets her talk for as long as she needs and will simply comment, '*I know, Rebecca*', and accept everything she says. It's not surprising that Rebecca feels reassured and valued and this has helped to reduce her anxiety, so that now she has fewer moments like these. Rebecca has also been able to find her sense of humour which we are all enjoying!

We discuss with staff their way of reacting to something and suggest other ways of coping, and we make sure we notice and comment if the person manages to do things more positively as a result. Everyone is working in an endless feedback loop. Everybody is happy to be part of this as long as the good things that are happening are highlighted and acknowledged alongside the struggles. We thank people for their help, hard work and commitment following difficult periods; for instance when Philip was badly burnt in an accident his team all worked extremely hard to support him while he was in hospital and to regain his and his family's trust: everyone was part of the recovery. We were clear in our feedback to everyone about how much their commitment had helped.

Noticing all of the subtle changes in people gives hope when things are difficult and motivates both staff and the supported person to keep on trying. For instance, for a long time when Matthew's team were trying to help him be brave enough to go out, the procedure would often get stuck at a point after he got dressed; he'd then get undressed on his way downstairs. But then the staff noticed he started to take time to look out of the window before he got undressed. This gave the team hope that he was interested in what was outside and that over time he might be interested enough to go out. As mentioned in an earlier chapter, this observation helped us to suggest to the men's group that they call at Matthew's house on the way to their meeting as a way of encouraging him to join them. They would all hang out in his front garden or in their cars beside his garden. We would say, *'Look, everyone's waiting for you and they all want you to join them'*. Gradually over time he ventured downstairs and got into his car and now Matthew is a fully participating member of the men's group. All of this work took years and was based on careful observation, feedback, hope – and the celebration of small steps.

Karl had been going to the same church for four and a half years when he managed to stay for the whole of the service for the first time. This was celebrated in the team meeting and his team were really excited for him; Karl was clearly proud of himself too. It is important to keep going with things. It's also important to help other people to, first, understand that it will take the person some time to learn and, second, to believe the person has the right to be present at such occasions and to take part in their own way. The congregation at the church have always welcomed Karl whether he stayed for five minutes or twenty. It was clear that Karl enjoyed the music and singing as well as being known and forming part of the community. Going to church helped Karl learn how and when he needs to listen, how to be quiet and how to belong to something.

Often we look in the wrong place to help people learn these important life skills. We had tried for a long time to support Karl in learning how to join in with things at college through a music course and a dance course. Sadly, the tutors never got beyond the fact that Karl wouldn't sit down and they couldn't see a way to include him and help him learn. People at the church he goes to have done this without any pressure or judgement; in fact he has been enabled to do it in his own way and has taught himself how to take part considerately. This shows the value in repeatedly showing up, in not giving up and in believing that the experience is helpful to the person however they approach it.

Encourage and support pride

Pride is an important component of celebration and belonging. You can be proud of what your organisation does and the difference it has made to people's lives. Good healthy pride is enhancing in a way that increases an individual's sense of self-worth and wellbeing. British people can be very cautious about feeling proud as we are good at seeing what has gone wrong with something rather than what is going right; I think 'Pride comes before a fall' is a message that is engrained deep in British culture. However, pride in yourself, your colleagues and the work you do, together with the people you support, is something people should feel good about and is affirming. We find that if staff members are supported to see progress in the people they work alongside, they talk with delight about their work and develop a pride in the organisation which is sometimes palpable.

Examples from our organisation are:

- Mark's pride in telling people, '*I have my own home now, I am independent now, and I can live in the community now*'.
- Veronica's pride in owning a dog.
- Minnie beaming and flapping her hands excitedly as she received her Oscar at the Oscars Night.
- Claire showing everyone her new clothes, shoes or boots.
- Karl's quiet pride when he sits on his horse at riding class.
- Angela's great excitement when we started to tell her about her gifts and talents, then her quiet listening as her gifts and talents were read to her, followed by her celebratory cheer and clapping as it ended.

- Minnie telling her team repeatedly that her home *'Is mine, this is mine'*.
- Matthew managing to spend the whole evening in his suit and new shoes at the Oscars Night.
- Philip sitting up and moving himself around on the floor while his team talked about his progress and his communication. He was visibly making himself bigger as he listened to the super feedback about himself.
- Patrick standing more upright and appearing much taller; he now walks tall instead of stooping.
- Catherine showing her pride when she has the reins in her hands and drives off in her carriage at her riding class.
- Karl taking visitors round his home when they visit, making sure they go in every room.
- Daniel's pride as he takes part in his cookery class and does most of the work himself; you can see by looking at him how much he is enjoying being competent.

Supporting people to be proud of themselves and their achievements is important both in terms of helping people be seen as people and less like victims, and in helping them become more powerful in their own right. Developing pride also enables people to be brave and to want more.

Catherine really wanted to dance with a man but rarely went to parties or celebrations where dancing happened. One day she did get to a party and a man helped her to dance. She was so proud and excited both by dancing and by dancing with a man that now she never misses a party and is always asking people to dance with her. Mark began to believe in his place in the world and to feel at home; he tells us he can live in the community and that he's proved it. Mark has since asked us to help him find some voluntary work in a school and to help him go on a cruise.

In staff appraisals we ask employees to reflect on something they've become proud of since working with us. We are always surprised by the range of things that they recognise. Some talk about the good relationship they have with the person they support or the person's family, some talk about a particular activity that they support the person in; this might be a holiday, perhaps a special time they had together, or a friendship or connection that they've helped the person to develop. Staff never struggle to think of things they are proud of in their job. This is heartening and keeps the people you support safer; staff who enjoy their jobs and have a pride in their work are much more likely to offer commitment and loyalty as well as effective support.

Knowing enough to care; sharing in the ups and downs

It's important not to get too hung up on confidentiality around sharing good and bad news within teams and with other teams. For there to be a real sense of belonging there has to be enough of a shared experience for someone to feel part of something. There is a mutual pride and excitement when something really special has happened for the people we support even if it isn't across the whole organisation: for example, all of the organisation got very excited and took great pleasure in sharing the celebrations of Daniel and Angela's relationship. Everyone was sad and upset when Philip had his accident. Another example of the caring and support shown across the whole organisation was visible when Angela had to go into hospital for several days. This was unexpected and a member of both her team and her partner Daniel's were on paternity leave at the same time. We were really struggling to support Angela in hospital and Daniel at home while also trying to enable him to visit her. Several staff from another team immediately offered to help as soon as they heard Angela was in hospital; this comes from a sense of belonging and shared concern which means everyone helps out in times of trouble. This is especially important when people are supported individually rather than in a communal situation; it helps to prevent the people supported and their team from feeling isolated.

Several years ago we discovered a large number of our staff would need to leave our employment as there were problems with their entitlement to live and work in Britain. After this happened it was important that we talked openly, being transparent about what had taken place and to help everyone understand what had occurred. This was the most painful and difficult time in our organisation; those involved had worked hard, paid tax and supported people very well. But legally they couldn't stay in our employ. When the staff were forced to leave we had the difficult task of talking to the people we support, the remaining staff and those newly recruited to offer them the opportunity to make sense of what had happened. We contracted Andy Smith and Pat Black from Diversity Matters to facilitate over these days, believing that it was important for someone independent of our organisation to help manage this, giving everyone the opportunity to talk openly about what had happened and how they felt. There was a lot of anger and distrust and a deep sadness. It has taken some time to heal and for everyone to trust again; it also took us a while to trust ourselves once more. We do recognise that out of difficult situations we are given the opportunity to learn a lot about ourselves, our principles, values and practices. We were also delighted to welcome back to work some of the staff once their entitlement to work here was established.

A great example of how to celebrate and show that we really see each other

Oscars Night
We held an Oscars Night at a stylish hotel. Everyone including their families and team members were invited. A red carpet led the way to the entrance which was flanked by two large Oscar statues, one either side. Everyone had their photos taken and we all walked through a balloon arch into the venue.

Everyone we support was awarded an Oscar. Each one was printed on plush paper and presented in a silver engraved napkin holder. These were read out over a microphone while being shown on a giant screen together with the person's photograph. Each person's Oscar was the result of lengthy reflection and based on insight gained from the person themselves, their support team and our observations.

There were also Oscars for every member of staff; these were displayed on the big screen while the band played. The team managers read these to each member of staff at their tables and presented them to people individually. They were read again in the team meetings following the Oscars Night, as were the ones for the person being supported. This created a wonderful sense of excitement and appreciation.

It was a great night, a stunning success and those family members who attended told us that they found it moving, amazing and enormous fun.

CHAPTER 9
Celebration and Belonging

KEY MESSAGES

- ☑ Celebrate what is happening and what is being achieved.
- ☑ Everyone is fine as they are, no one needs fixing.
- ☑ Make time to notice and then celebrate and appreciate the person.
- ☑ Share good news and success stories amongst other support teams within the organisation.
- ☑ Be positive.
- ☑ The culture and practice of celebrating and valuing people makes people safer.
- ☑ Re-discover pride and give permission for people to be proud.
- ☑ People are happier when they are valued.
- ☑ When people feel seen a sense of safety emerges and the right conditions arise for personal growth.

Chapter 10

Are Getta Life Doing What They Say?

Evidence gathered through testimony:
the voice of external professionals,
presented by Jack Richardson
of True 2 Self

It was at my instigation that we included the testimonies in this last chapter because I was concerned that, for many readers, Getta Life could seem to be too good to be true. I felt that some external validation was needed to prove that they do, indeed, achieve what they outline in the rest of the book. For myself, I can only say that what I've witnessed in the time I've been working alongside Sue and Julie has had a profound effect on me and on my own expectations, perceptions and, yes, prejudices about supporting people with learning difficulties. I feel I've been privileged to witness how people have been helped at the most far-reaching level, and led to appreciate that they are worthwhile people like any others with gifts and talents and an ability to both contribute to and benefit from society. Recognising this, and acting in a way that promotes it so successfully, is the strength of Getta Life. I hope it's an inspiration.

Most of us who work in the arena of providing support to others will, I suspect, hold similar values and beliefs based around treating people fairly, with respect, dignity and compassion. We are naturally drawn to the support organisations that align themselves with our beliefs and values. Sometimes we can be drawn in by well-written promises or usage of current terminology or perhaps slick advertising. Yet most of us become aware very quickly if we've been misled. When that's the case, the reality is not one of an actively caring organisation, but more likely to be one which places heavy emphasis on tasks and safeguarding: one where the people being supported are not truly seen or listened to, let alone encouraged to live their dreams and aspirations.

So what makes Getta Life different from most providers offering support? It's simple. Getta Life is not motivated by empire-building, or financial reward. They haven't built up their organisation through smart advertising but by word of mouth.

This book sets out to show what makes Getta Life different from most providers offering support to people with learning difficulties while offering insight and tools to other providers. Yet so far, the reader has had only the word of people from Getta Life and Diversity Matters that the organisation is meeting its own high standards and that the people they support are receiving this in the way they state. Sue and Julie, the founders of Getta Life, feel that it is important to offer external evidence in corroboration.

So in this chapter we offer evidence gathered through testimony from external professionals via surveys and interviews. We also talk to people more closely attached to Getta Life, such as parents and a supporter of the organisation. Below is a record of this testimony with a clarification of each interviewee's relationship to Getta Life, and inclusion of the questions we asked so the answers can be read in context.

The voice of external professionals

1. Mark Baxter, Consultant Psychiatrist

How do you know Getta Life?

> I have known Getta Life for several years in their capacity as service providers for a number of my clients. I have seen them provide for clients and enable them to move out of long-stay hospital care, to enjoy rich and fulfilling lives in the community.

What has been your experience of Getta Life?

> This has been extremely positive. The organisation has a high set of values that are clearly understood by all the staff whom I have met. They have been able to support clients in a way that I did not think was possible and they have been extremely successful.

Your opinion of what Getta Life does?

> Getta Life is by far the best independent sector provider that I have come across. Clients' lives are simply transformed.

2. John Kavanagh, Director of Open Doors Housing & Support Ltd

In what capacity do you know Sue and Julie of Getta Life?

> I have worked with Julie and Sue for the best part of twenty years. We first worked together while I was a manager in Coventry City Council's Community Education Department, when we developed and implemented community-based educational programmes and qualifications for people with learning disabilities. A priority was that the people we worked with should be at the centre of our work.
>
> Along with enlightened and passionate City Council managers, at the time we began to work in partnership to plan the exciting process of supporting people to move from traditional residential care to living in their own homes. Many of these people had become excluded and isolated from society.

Could you briefly describe what it's like working with Sue and Julie?

> It's inspirational. Julie and Sue are and always have been passionate about what they do, they respect and value their clients totally; they will not accept second best. They have demonstrated beyond doubt, and on numerous occasions, that supported living can work for anyone. They lead by example and have not drifted away from day-to-day contact with their clients. Their in-house training is excellent and emanates their values.

How would you describe Getta Life to others?

> The best there is! If I had a family member who required support I would be fighting for Getta Life to provide the support. They set the benchmark for person-centred work and best practice in supported living.

Anything else you would like to add?

> Words are difficult to do justice to Getta Life, their clients and staff. If, like me, you were lucky enough to attend a Getta Life annual celebration evening in full flow and witnessed the vitality, happiness, pride and achievement that is there in abundance amongst clients, family and staff, often in the face of the most difficult and damning circumstances, your faith in mankind, people's possibilities and the human spirit would be inestimably lifted!

3. **Catherine Nolan, Joint Strategic Commissioner for People with Disabilities, Business Transformation Directorate at Solihull Metropolitan Borough Council**

In what capacity do you know Sue and Julie of Getta Life?

> We met over twenty years ago when we were all working in Coventry with people with learning difficulties. Sue was a community learning disability nurse, Julie was managing a specific service within the NHS and I was managing a support service in social services. We were bound together in our belief in the rights of people with learning difficulties and I knew they were going to do something very special.
>
> Now my relationship with them is that of a service commissioner and they support a number of Solihull people for us, and do it superbly.

Could you briefly describe what it's like working with them?

> Well, of course I know them well and like them, so my answer is necessarily from that perspective. I find it very easy: it's focused on the person at the heart of things, and very solution-centred and practical, i.e. what do we need to do to get this sorted/resolved/moving/fixed?

How would you describe Getta Life to others?

> I describe Getta Life as the most effective, person-centred, values-driven and skilled organisation I work with. They're not remotely fazed by the 'reputations' of people they may be asked to support. They are passionate yet pragmatic, skilled yet sensitive, driven and inspiring.

4. Molly Mattingly, Head of Learning Disability Programmes, Foundation for People with Learning Disabilities

In what capacity do you know Sue and Julie of Getta Life?

> I have known Sue and Getta Life since 2006. They participated in the Foundation's three-year project called 'Life in the Community', funded through the Mental Health Foundation and Bailey Thomas funds. Through this research project they learnt the best ways for people with significant needs to develop more relationships with community members and how supporting them to do this might best be accomplished. In April 2012 we were asked to put a proposal together to evaluate Getta Life using quality outcome measures, added value, value for money and how they best meet government guidance on supporting people who challenge services. During the evaluation my colleagues and I got to spend a lot of time with Sue and Julie, together with the people they support, their families and the Getta Life staff. It is the first time in my experience that I could actually see, feel, hear and sense the love, commitment, empathy and passion for people with learning disabilities, and their families, and those who support them.

Could you briefly describe what it's like working with them?

> Extremely positive and enlightening, and hopeful in the sense that if they can do it, others can! They are people who can see the challenges and barriers yet are not intimidated by them, as they're grounded in their values and beliefs which promote the positive capabilities and images of people with learning disabilities.
>
> They are willing to take on new ideas and participate in discussions about new ways of looking at things both internally and externally. Their leadership styles are different, yet they complement each other. However, both demonstrate a supportive, coaching, mentor style of management. They are extremely welcoming and hospitable to all those who want to be part of the organisation. They don't assume fuzzy styles of leadership but are clear in their vision about how the organisation will support people with learning disabilities, their families and supporters. When they don't agree with feedback it's done in a respectful way and in a conversational style. Both Julie and Sue are best at informality, yet if formality is needed it's undertaken in a professional manner.

How would you describe Getta Life to others?

> As the best provider of supported living services to people with disabilities, their families and support workers. Getta Life do what they say and go beyond 'good' support to 'excellent' support. They are passionate and committed. They recruit and train a skilled and knowledgeable workforce of people who are also empathetic, compassionate, flexible and respectful. They lead by example. They love the people they work with and for. They are a family! They are the model which all services should use as the baseline!

Anything else you would like to add?

> They truly love and care about people with learning disabilities and their families. They see their gifts, talents and capabilities first! I have been privileged to spend time with everyone in the organisation.

5. Steve Jones, Learning Disability Team Manager

In what capacity do you know Sue and Julie of Getta Life?

> I've known Sue since the late 1980s and Julie for the past ten years. My first connection with Getta Life was when they were selected to provide the support for Elizabeth Mews and I was the project lead. I have also worked for them for the last twelve months as an independent person-centred planner.

Could you briefly describe what it's like working with them?

It's fun – good fun – working with them. One of the things I like about their working style is it's always so reflective. There's a lot of seat-of-the-pants stuff, 'Let's do this, let's see how it goes', and then there's the reflection and then there's 'Well that didn't quite work did it, let's try it a different way'. There's no ego; there's no, 'We are the best at this', it's actually about saying 'Well that didn't feel right' or 'That's been the right thing for that person'. There's lots of feelings stuff which is very much a part of my social work experience, and which I'm not always sure is there for everybody these days. It shouldn't just be about 'Let's get this done' and 'What are the outcomes?' and all the rest of it, it should also be about 'How did that feel?'. So the really strong combination of values and beliefs, and the being reflective and actually working on your own feelings, characterises what it's like working with them. And that's why I enjoy it so much.

How would you describe Getta Life to others?

I've had to do this in fact. If I'm trying to do it simply, it's talking about their support for people and their attention to detail and their respect for people.
Then I normally end up talking about Sue and Julie themselves, because they have a strong view that good support comes from small organisations, where people in the organisation are always involved with the people they are supporting, and I absolutely agree with that. As most people will realise, any support service is only as good as the people who manage and work within it. That's what I tend to talk about. Invariably I'm talking to families, and families understand things through people, they're not interested in organisations per se; they're interested in the people who support their sons and daughters – people like Sue and Julie.

What are the differences in what Getta Life are achieving compared with the majority of people you are in contact with who are trying to do the same thing?

> Well, there are lots of other support organisations that do achieve similar things to Getta Life but they don't get quite as far, and of course they're not necessarily working with such complex people. But I suppose the major difference for me is Getta Life's attention to detail and the fact they're always moving forward with the people they support, and even though it can be a lengthy process, people are achieving more over longer periods of time. It's been interesting for me when I've been doing person-centred planning with Getta Life. The last couple of planning days that I've done have been with relatively new people who are only a year or two into being supported by Getta Life. Getta Life have clearly made a big difference, and yet I'm saying to families, 'Well actually it's early days; some of the people I've been seeing have been supported for six or seven years and Getta Life are still working to learn even more about them, and those people are still achieving and moving forward and becoming more settled and happy'. So after just one or two years, even though there have been great developments, it's not the end yet.

Anything else you would like to add?

> I know that I'm not alone in this view as I've spoken to plenty of other workers: any individual who ends up being supported by Getta Life is very lucky. As a worker, if you're able to secure Getta Life as your support organisation you just feel that you've opened up somebody's life to huge amounts of joy and happiness.
>
> As a social worker it's the most wonderful feeling. You've met someone, you've done your assessment, you've met the family, you've taken on board all of their anxieties and expectations as well as all of the things that they would like to see happen – and invariably the feeling is, we need Getta Life. But you know you can't have them necessarily, so that when you do achieve that it's a lovely feeling, it's like giving someone this huge ongoing Christmas present.

The voice of those close to the people being supported

1. **Marjorie Sargeant – part of a circle of friends of a person supported by Getta Life.**

   How do you see the impact of Getta Life on the individuals being supported?

   > People have become individuals with an identity, rights, choices, status. They are valued and respected and are now people in their own right, in their own home and in their own community.
   >
   > I have seen individual personalities emerge, each with individual styles, abilities, learning, skills and talents, relationships and lifestyles.

   In your opinion what does Getta Life do?

   > Getta Life supports people:
   > - to be their own selves and be recognised as such;
   > - to be valued people in their own home and community;
   > - to have the same rights and opportunities as everyone else;
   > - to be respected and valued for themselves and who they are;
   > - to be loved;
   > - to be a friend;
   > - to be able to give as well as receive;
   > - to choose;
   > - to be cared for according to their needs.
   >
   > Getta Life gives a quality service with professional integrity and high standards of care, support and training. They are responsible, accountable and transparent. The people they support are always central to the action.

2. Justin's mum and dad

> Before Getta Life we were advised that Justin should go to an assessment unit. We felt there was a danger of him being locked up and his life would have ended. Getta Life have enabled him to lead an interesting and fulfilled life. He does what he wants and is beginning to take control, all while being supported in a safe and sensitive way.

In your opinion what does Getta Life do?

> - Values and respects people, clients and staff.
> - Empathises and tries to work out why people react in certain ways and how they feel.
> - Supports choice and decision-making.
> - Accepts people how they are.
> - Supports staff and provides extensive training.
> - Has the ethos and attitudes to support people with high levels of need.

3. **Daniel's mother**

> My experience of Getta Life has been eye-opening. They have given me hope and eased my worries. I now know that my son feels worthwhile, is happy and enjoying life.

How do you see the impact of Getta Life on the individuals being supported?

> Almost unbelievable! Through the hard work and dedication of everyone at Getta Life each individual now has a purpose in life. They are able to learn to do something more each day and to be happy.

In your opinion what does Getta Life do?

> With care, sympathy and patience, Getta Life transforms every individual who maybe feels lonely or bewildered into someone who gradually finds that their life is now exciting, fun, interesting and full of possibilities. Speaking on behalf of my son I would like to offer a heartfelt thank you to everyone at Getta Life.